PRAXEOLOGY

The invisible hand that feeds you

Knut Svanholm

Edited by Mel Shilling & Niko Laamanen

KONSENSUS NETWORK

© 2023 Knut Svanholm

All rights reserved.

Edited by Mel Shilling & Niko Laamanen

Cover design by Knut Svanholm & Niko Laamanen

Typesetting by Gonzalo Coelho & Niko Laamanen

ISBN 978-9916-723-05-0 Hardcover

　　978-9916-723-06-7 Paperback

　　978-9916-723-07-4 Ebook

PRESS ★ https://konsensus.network

Contents

Foreword		v
1	ACTION	1
2	MEANS AND ENDS	9
3	RETURNS	15
4	LABOR	21
5	CAPITAL, TIME AND TRADE	27
6	MONEY	35
7	MARKETS	43
8	COMPETITION	51
9	ENTREPRENEURSHIP	59
10	PROGRESS	65
11	PRICES	71
12	PURCHASING POWER	79
13	TIME PREFERENCE	85
14	LOANS AND INTEREST	93
15	CAPITAL THEORY	99
16	COUNTERFEITING	107
17	ARGUMENTATION	113
18	CONCLUSION	119
Further Reading		121

Foreword

Who would author a book on a tongue-twisting term that eludes the comprehension of most? Knut Svanholm! True, economists are known for their penchant for complex jargon, but Knut is far from your conventional economist, and his work is no ordinary introduction to the field. The term "praxeology" was proposed by Ludwig von Mises in an effort to distance himself from modern economics. While the word "economics" shares a similarly enigmatic Greek heritage, it has become more prevalent, albeit for all the wrong reasons: Economics has metamorphosed into a widespread charade spanning centuries, amassing wealth and influence for self-proclaimed "economists." The term projects an aura of scientific rigor, financial prowess, and expert counsel, yet its origins reveal a nefarious intent.

In Ancient Greece, oikonomía was the art of pragmatic household management. Imagine Socrates and Plato engaged in a spirited conversation over a glass of wine, exchanging insights on the optimal ways to oversee their wives, slaves, and livestock. During the era of absolutist mercantilism, the concept evolved to encompass the belief that a paternalistic ruler should similarly govern "his" political dominions, maximizing the productivity of "his" human resources. As modern governance emerged, paternal affection dissipated, and the primary objective became the augmentation of wealth and authority for those in managerial and expert roles. It is thus no wonder that the Soviet Union, with its bureaucratic machinery, boasted the highest proportion of economists among its workforce in history.

Praxeologists, by contrast, approach human beings on a more equitable basis. We may not consistently act in an economical or economizing manner, but we must all make choices, employing uncertain means to achieve our varied and subjective goals. Admittedly, the term "praxeology," translating to the "logic of human action," may be somewhat ambitious. One could fill volumes on either "logic" or "human action" – indeed, Ludwig von Mises' magnum opus bears the very title Human Action. In this context, "logic" or "science" refers to a systematic study employing reason while diligently circumventing fallacies, biases, and personal interests that could otherwise obscure our judgment.

In an age where trusting one's own reason is often viewed as contrarian, praxeology has occasionally been labeled dogmatic. This characterization, however, is far from accurate. In his old Vienna circle, Ludwig von Mises encouraged critical discourse and refrained from adopting the persona of a prophetic guru. In his seminal work, Human Action, Mises acknowledges that he "can never be absolutely certain that his inquiries were not misled and that what he considers as certain truth is not error." Consequently, he emphasizes the importance of subjecting his theories to continuous critical reexamination. This intellectual humility starkly contrasts the contemporary landscape, where so-called "scientific experts" readily lend their prestige to politicians, empowering them to "fix" the lives of others while struggling to maintain order in their own affairs.

The Austrian School of Economics has always championed an open-minded approach, neither sanctioning nor censoring any research method. Ironically, it was the proponents of the once-dominant historicism and later positivism who sought to marginalize praxeology within the economic profession and academia. At its core, praxeology embraces the intricacies of human phenomena, acknowledging that real human beings are prone to error, capable of learning and adapting, driven by subjective desires, and compelled to make choices. This unwavering commitment to realism is often misconstrued as axiomatic dogmatism.

Praxeology does not attempt to predict the future state of the world through a priori axioms. Instead, it employs deduction to distill core insights from human reality into a skeletal yet universal framework, unbiased and clear, while remaining sufficiently meaningful to facilitate the interpretation of data. Admittedly, much of contemporary "Austrian Economics" is characterized by repurposing second-hand ideas for ideological conflicts. However, it would be unjust to attribute this to praxeology itself. The fact that Mises championed liberty is not a shortcoming but a testament to his virtue.

Praxeology aims to sidestep another pervasive danger inherent in economics. In an era dominated by short-term materialism, the prevailing mantra is: It's the economy, stupid! Consequently, the focus narrows to the pursuit of money – not merely acquiring wealth but amassing ever-increasing fortunes. This mindset, far from being a praxeological axiom, is symptomatic of a distorted monetary system. The concept of "making money" has come to signify outpacing the Cantillon effect (a crucial notion explored in this book). The primary objective of "making money" is no longer centered around delivering value to others or performing one's job with diligence and efficiency. Instead, it has devolved into a relentless race to multiply existing wealth faster than it loses purchasing power.

This artificially induced financial frenzy greatly benefits another facet of the "economics" charade — generating demand for "market expertise" that bears no connection to genuine proficiency in real markets. This misguided masquerade involves inflating asset values under the guise of financial advice. These "applied" economists rarely face accountability for their predictions. If one were to apply mainstream economics to itself, the scarcity of empirical evidence or credible models supporting its purported predictive prowess would be astonishing. In reality, entrusting one's fate to the roll of the dice may prove a far safer gamble than heeding the investment counsel of economists.

Far more crucial than individual wealth is the "wealth of nations," humanity's transition from the Malthusian trap to the leisure that underpins higher culture. This is the foundational question addressed by the most developed branch of praxeology: *catallactics*. The etymology of this perplexing term is delightfully charming, originating from a Greek verb meaning both exchange and transforming foes into friends. Catallactics seeks to comprehend why and how cooperation between strangers forges enduring societal bonds, shifting from zero-sum redistribution to positive-sum wealth creation. It begins with the humility of marveling at the miracle of decentralized production rather than taking its fruits for granted. Frédéric

Bastiat, an early praxeologist and opponent of French absolutism, referred to this phenomenon as the miracle of "Paris being fed." The accomplishment is not the work of a single invisible hand but the coordination of millions of visible, industrious hands—invisible only to the privileged Parisian who views his sustenance as a birthright. Early economists, ensconced in the grand palaces of the powerful, failed to appreciate this miracle, perceiving bountiful goods as preexisting resources merely awaiting distribution to deserving recipients. For them, the matter was one of palace logistics, akin to the temple economy overseen by ancient god-kings.

Ludwig von Mises recognized that neither human rights, paper edicts, nor intellectual trends could guarantee the sustenance of millions who reside in crowded cities, far removed from farmlands, due to the division of labor and protection against marauding invaders. He successfully averted a blockade of Vienna that would have doomed its inhabitants to starvation. More significantly, he contributed to the argument against the central planning responsible for claiming millions of lives in the 20th century. Catallactics leads to an appreciation of peaceful and borderless human collaboration, not out of sentimentality or a desire to "save humanity," but through an understanding of the logic underpinning positive-sum exchange.

Alas, most economic intuitions still adhere to the archaic zero-sum mindset. A majority of academic economics continues to focus on the allocation of goods and services, with its mercantilist "balances of trade," "optimal" taxes, and expert interventions to address "market failure." Ultimately, these notions perpetuate the fallacy of a caste of rational palace economists presiding over an irrational populace.

To all that, the study of praxeology offers a refreshing reprieve: a humble inquiry into the acts of real human beings like you and me, devoid of the pretensions associated with exact formulas, elite influence, and get-rich-quick stratagems. In an increasingly crazy world of make-believe, grant yourself some much-needed respite and delight in accompanying Knut on a captivating journey down the praxeological rabbit hole.

Rahim Taghizadegan, April 13th 2023
(Last Austrian praxeologist in the direct tradition)

Don't bite the invisible hand that feeds you.

"I learned to look more upon the bright side of my condition, and less upon the dark side, and to consider what I enjoyed, rather than what I wanted: and this gave me sometimes such secret comforts, that I cannot express them; and which I take notice of here, to put those discontented people in mind of it, who cannot enjoy comfortably what God has given them, because they see and covet something that he has not given them. All our discontents about what we want appeared to me to spring from the want of thankfulness for what we have."

– Daniel Defoe, The Life and Adventures of Robinson Crusoe

1

ACTION

SCIENCE is a systematic endeavor that builds and organizes knowledge through testable explanations and predictions about our world. Most sciences taught in schools can be called *a-posteriori* sciences — sciences that arrive at conclusions from empirical testing. While these sciences can be helpful, they only provide us with models of how things work and never accurately describe reality. The map can never be the territory. A precise model of the universe would have to be the universe itself. But there is another subset of science called *a-priori* science. *A-priori* knowledge refers to things that can be known independently of experience using deductive reasoning alone. Mathematics is the most obvious example of a branch of science that can be classified as *a-priori*. Mathematics describes objective reality, and it exists regardless of people's individual interpretations of its implications. Reason alone can tell why two plus two equals four, and no empirical testing is required to arrive at that conclusion.

Apart from mathematics, there's another branch of *a-priori* science relatively unknown to most people. It is called *Praxeology* — the science of deliberate human action. Praxeology is to the subjective what mathematics is to the objective. Most people, including most scientists, believe social sciences belong to the realm of *a-posteriori* knowledge. But this is not the case if you accept a particular set of self-evident axioms about human beings to be true. Robinson Crusoe, when first marooned on the island, has to do a lot of empirical, a-posteriori research to figure out what kind of situation he's in. He doesn't know whether the island is inhabited, whether there are wild beasts to worry about, let alone whether he's on an island at all. But he does have some a-priori knowledge to help him figure things out. He can tell that the grass on the island is green by observing it, but he knows that green is a color *a-priori* to the observation.

Critics of praxeology have argued that because praxeology rejects positivism and empiricism in the development of theories, it constitutes nothing less than a rejection of the scientific method. They claim this rejection invalidates the a-priori deductive reasoning methodology, rendering praxeology, the study of human action and conduct, inadequate to describe economics. Praxeologists, conversely, argue that it is a-posteriori reasoning and empirical evidence-based testing that is insufficient to describe economics. Ludwig von Mises, in particular, argued against empiricist approaches to the social sciences in general because human events are unique and non-repeatable. In contrast, experiments in the physical sciences are necessarily reproducible. Are all social sciences, therefore, wrong? Well, if they arrive at conclusions empirically, yes. Human beings have *autonomy* and thus cannot be studied in the same way as gravity, fluids, or magnetism. Empirical social sciences are always at risk of falling into the trap of political bias. How experiments are conducted, what groups to study, and even what to focus on in the first place are always products of the evaluations of a single human mind. Praxeologists strive to remove these biases entirely by admitting that individuals are decision-makers and that anything that involves purposeful behavior (or *human action*) can only be studied by logical deduction from a set of irrefutable axioms.

Consequently, empirical data cannot falsify economic theory nor predict or explain human action. A case can be made that a-priori sciences are more robust and, therefore, necessarily more accurate and truthful than a-posteriori ones. Empirical evidence can give us good guesses of how the world actually works. Still, a-priori deductive reasoning cannot be argued against and is thus more factual on an even deeper level. In philosophy and science, a *first principle* is a basic assumption that cannot be deduced from any other proposition or assumption. In mathematics, first principles are referred to as *axioms*. "First-principles thinking" means deriving things to their fundamental, proven axioms in the given arena. Only after doing this can you come to conclusions that do not violate any fundamental laws.

The laws of human action are necessarily true and universal because they're logically implied by simple, indisputable facts. In arguing against these facts, you prove them to be true. One example would be the fact that you control your own body. In arguing against this fact, you must use your vocal cords, tongue, and lips to make sounds that form words and sentences. In doing so, you must control them, thereby proving yourself wrong. Knowing the basics of praxeology is crucial to understanding the world you live in, and it can fundamentally change how you choose to spend the days you still have left on this Earth. Praxeological axioms are timeless truths applicable to all human beings, regardless of sex, race, creed, or color. The starting point of praxeology is one such axiom: Human action is purposeful behavior. Refuting this argument would require you to act with an intended purpose — to argue against a self-evident statement. In doing so, you prove that same statement to be true. Once we accept the self-evident axioms of praxeology to be accurate, we can discover other implied truths. They can provide us with a lens through which we can view the world of human beings and see it as it truly is. Finding these truths is what praxeology is all about. An unbiased way to understand the phenomena humans call economics, politics, nation-states, religions, war, and peace. Understanding humans and human action without holding opinions about them and their behavior.

Human action is purposeful behavior. In other words, deliberately aiming at ends and goals. Unconscious behavior, such as by reflex removing your hand from a hot surface, does not count as human action. Spasms, reflexes, sleepwalking, and other unconscious behaviors lay outside the realm of praxeology. So do the instinctual behaviors of animals, weather phenomena, and other things outside of a person's control. An acting individual must, however, consider things outside their control when acting purposefully. However, praxeology is the study of the action itself, not the psychological events that led the person to operate with intent. Praxeology omits analysis of the individual actor's motive. An acting individual chooses, determines, and attempts to reach a desired end. There is also a temporal element to human action since most actions cannot happen simultaneously. Every human being must act. Every human being must evaluate their options at every given moment and choose what to do next. Equally important is perceived human *inaction*. Purposeful inaction also counts as action in a praxeological sense. For instance, saving money for later use doesn't require you to do anything but wait. But it is still purposeful behavior. Thus saving is a human action. Purposeful behavior distinguishes humans from other animals and allows for civilization to arise.

Human action always aims at altering one's environment into a more satisfactory state. Even the most trivial human action can be described as an exchange between what we could have done and what we actually do. We always trade with ourselves and choose one action over another, just like when we choose one product or service over another when engaged in trade with other human beings. The only psychological prerequisite for triggering purposeful action in human beings is an eagerness to *remove a felt uneasiness* in one's mind. When a human mind perceives reality to be unsatisfactory in some way, that human chooses to act. The mind imagines its future environment, sees how it could become more satisfactory, values one action over others, and acts accordingly.

In short, three things happen in our minds before we choose to act. First, we find ourselves in a state of uneasiness. Secondly, we imagine a world without this uneasiness, and finally, an idea arises — a belief that a particular action can quell the uneasiness. Then, and only then, we act purposefully, with intent. If you remove one of these three, no action will take place. A person who does not feel uncomfortable or uneasy will not do anything. For instance, a junkie amid a chemically induced bliss has no reason to act. If you remove one of the two latter states — in other words, if a human lacks the imagination to envision the world in a more satisfactory state because of their actions — they won't act. Put another way — human action is the pursuit of happiness, a state of mind that can only occur when all the things one is unhappy with have been removed.

The study of human action from first principles must be absolutely rigid and logically correct if it is to be helpful in our understanding of the world around us. Praxeology does not engross whatever subjective imagined future a human thinks will make them happy. It only concerns itself with action and the logic that governs it. What makes a man happy, satisfied, or uneasy is no concern to the study of purposeful action itself. If the praxeologist were to weigh these things, the study would inevitably become biased and opinionated. In this sense, people's personal goals are of no concern to praxeology as a science. It doesn't matter whether you're a dictator trying to relieve yourself of a state of uneasiness by invading another country, a rockstar trying to become happy by having sex with groupies, or a volunteer for a charity project trying to feel better by "doing good," we all act because we believe our actions will alleviate our uneasiness. We can always do something else if our efforts do not satisfy us. We choose between a current set of available actions at every given moment.

Even in very emotional states, we can, to some extent, act upon our instincts or quell them and choose a more diplomatic route. For instance, when arguing with your spouse, you can give in to the urge to walk out of the room and slam the door shut or take a deep breath and say, "I hear what you're saying, darling." Before choosing one before the other and actually doing something, we feel uneasy and imagine how our spouse will react to each available action. Only then do we choose whatever action we believe will lead to the least bad outcome. The critical thing to remember is that we always have a hierarchy of wants and wishes in our minds and always choose one action above all others at each given moment. This "value hierarchy" and our mind's reaction to it always precedes every deliberate action. Action is always necessarily *rational* because an acting person cannot act without aiming toward a specific goal. In praxeology, the word "rational" means "purposeful" and has nothing to do with how intelligent or reasonable the action may seem to a subjective observer. Whether an observer views a specific action as sensible does not matter. Rational implies that the actor reasoned themselves to a conclusion that led to their subsequent step — an action. Whether that decision was *sensible* or not is someone's opinion. Opinions can not be explained from deductive reasoning based on irrefutable axioms. By deeming someone else's action *irrational*, you point out that you would have done otherwise had you been in that person's shoes.

From the perspective of the individual doing it, however, the decision was made intentionally and is, hence, rational. It is impossible to put oneself in someone else's shoes entirely and, therefore, impossible to fully understand another human being's true motives. Praxeology illuminates this philosophical insight and helps us establish the boundaries of knowledge about other human beings. We can, in fact, never know the true motives behind another human's actions. Praxeology acknowledges that human beings have free will, which we ironically have no choice but to have if we are to understand anything about the world around us.

Praxeology uses logic to examine the means chosen to attain specific ends sought by the actor and the implications of selecting certain means over others.

"I have been, in all my circumstances, a memento to those who are touched with the general plague of mankind, whence, for aught I know, one half of their miseries flow: I mean that of not being satisfied with the station wherein God and Nature hath placed them."

– Daniel Defoe, *The Life and Adventures of Robinson Crusoe*

2

MEANS AND ENDS

To act purposefully is to try to reach certain ends through means, consciously. Praxeology refers to an end as an imagined state of the world without a particular felt uneasiness. A human being must employ a means to reach this desired end. A thing becomes a means when human reason plans to use it to attain an end. The term "letting the ends justify the means" makes little sense praxeologically since means not already justified by a person's desired ends cannot exist. Means are constructs of the human mind and couldn't exist without us. Whether to consider a physical object a means is entirely up to the individual actor trying to reach a particular end. A roadblock can provide a perfect means to a person wishing to block off a road, but that same roadblock acts as an obstacle to a person trying to drive past it.

Praxeology is the study of man's relationship with the world around him. It is not the study of objects in the physical realm, nor is it the study of entirely subjective psychological phenomena. It studies how the two realities relate to one another through human action. Praxeology remains devoid of value judgments by not analyzing people's ultimate goals but instead studying the concepts of means and ends. It cannot tell us much about *why* humans act but rather explores what happens when a person *does* act. For instance, praxeological deductive reasoning alone can teach us a lot about how an increase in a society's money supply affects its inhabitant's incentives. It can't tell us anything about percentages or to what extent people will act because of these incentives, but we can figure out why this is unknowable through praxeological reasoning. It can also teach us how free market interventions inevitably lead to resource misallocation. All this knowledge stems from the fact that a person's value judgment is entirely subjective and dynamic. Accepting this basic fact about humans unlocks a plethora of insights. These insights lead to conclusions that people never arrive at if they falsely believe that value can be intrinsic to physical objects.

At every given moment, a person chooses between a set of actions. What action the person chooses depends on what ends they seek and what means they believe will bring them to those ends most efficiently. The act demonstrates the actor's value judgment and which option they deem most valuable to reach their goals at that moment. In other words, it shows how the actor weighs their alternatives. The fact that there's a choice involved implies that we can build a scale referencing an actor's values.

If Robinson Crusoe goes fishing in a freshwater pond at a particular time, we can conclude that at that specific moment, he prefers going fishing over staying at home. Every action correlates perfectly with a person's scale of values because the scale is just a tool for logically interpreting a person's action. The only way of determining how a conscious actor values one thing above another is by observing how they act.

Now imagine that he already had a fish in his hut and chose to stay home and cook it instead. We cannot know how this choice was made in this case because, in this case, Robinson never faced the initial dilemma of whether to go fishing or stay at home but instead faced a different one — whether to go fishing or stay at home and cook the fish he had already caught. We cannot know whether he would have preferred going fishing or staying at home had he not already acquired a fish. Only by observing action can we establish what a person finds more critical. We show how we value things by reacting to our environment's conditions. A person can claim to cherish one thing above another, but action speaks louder than words. Only by acting can we change the world around us.

As explained, human beings act to alter the world around them to better suit their wants and needs. The concept of change implies a temporal order to human action. Action implies time. We must constantly choose what activity to engage in first because everything we do requires time. In praxeology, the terms past, present, and future are defined as the time before, during, and after the action. Chained to the unforgiving arrow of time, humans always aim their actions toward the future. In a praxeological sense, action always occurs in the present. In a strict physics sense, "the present" refers to a particular point in space-time. To the individual acting human being, the present is a prolonged period during which the action occurs. In this sense, "the present" includes identifying an uneasiness, creating a plan to remove it, and finally doing something to reach that goal. The anxiety a human feels will continue until that human takes action and tries to remove it.

Time is different from all other physical goods and services since time can never be abundant and thus is always costly to spend doing something rather than something else. In other words — human time is always scarce. We must economize our time whenever we act, just as we must economize all other scarce resources. Even if everything else were superabundant and free, like air, every person would still need to economize their time. And temporally, you could still only do one thing at a time. Even in a world where everything comes without cost or effort, everyone must choose what to consume first. No one can eat, sleep, walk the dog, and read a book simultaneously. Actions can happen in rapid succession, but praxeology does not allow multitasking. An action can serve multiple purposes. But between two actions, one must always necessarily follow the other.

It is important to note that a specific value scale only applies to one action at a time. The fact that two actions cannot be performed simultaneously by one individual logically implies that actions are independent of one another concerning their scale of value. The scale of value is merely a tool for an observer to use to make sense of another person's actions. If a person prefers bananas to apples and apples to oranges at one time, that person may still choose an orange over a banana at another time. Value scales are always dynamic; the acting person's reality changes with each subsequent event. Circumstances, people, and their relationships with one another change over time. The way humans experience time in this sense shows that mathematical predictions of human behavior can only ever give us flawed models of the future. Every person on Earth strives for a state of less uneasiness, and everyone has to consider the scarcity of time when trying to reach their goals.

Action implies uncertainty about the future. If the universe was deterministic, and one could predict everything with absolute certainty, one wouldn't ever need to choose; therefore, one wouldn't need to act. Without choice, life would be a movie rather than a computer game. In this hypothetical world, we would only *react* to external stimuli and never act out our free will. The natural sciences, in general, and physics, in particular, can predict what will happen in the future after a definite set of events. But they can't foresee things about nature that we haven't yet figured out, nor how humans will act of their own free will. One phenomenon physics can teach us about is entropy. Entropy is a scientific concept (as well as a measurable physical property) most commonly associated with a state of disorder, randomness, or uncertainty. In a deterministic universe, that is, a universe in which free will couldn't exist, entropy wouldn't exist. So physics has, in this sense, a-priori proven that free will *can* exist by introducing us to the phenomenon of entropy.

We can interact with the future in three different ways — we can gamble, speculate, or engineer. All human action falls under one or more of these subcategories. When we gamble, we can calculate whether the odds are in our favor, but we must rely on luck for each specific event. When we speculate, we adjust our efforts based on our ability to foresee the future. We reduce the risk involved by gathering information about the outcome. Every human action is a form of speculation. When we engineer, we use the tools and knowledge about the world around us to achieve our desired ends. We reduce risk by taking precautions and safety measures. In praxeological terms, engineering means striving to gain complete control over the elements of action. Since human beings have different goals and desires, no one can engineer society. The will of a political leader, like a president or a prime minister, can never replace the wants and needs of an individual human being. An individual must believe that whatever means he chooses at any given moment will bring him closer to his desired ends, and no leader can force that belief. Politics can influence people's thoughts, but a human being can never fully function as a mere cog in another human's machine. One can engineer an army of robots, but one cannot socially engineer entities that act by their own free will.

Praxeology can help us predict future outcomes of action, but there are limits to what we can know. For instance, we can, with logical certainty, say that a fall in demand for a good will lead to a drop in the price of that good, given that all other factors remain unchanged. We can, however, never predict *how much* the price will drop. We can never imply anything quantitative. Human value scales are ordinal and not cardinal, so we can never apply mathematical models to predict human behavior. Our prediction can lead to a logical set of outcomes, but these expected outcomes can only be qualitative, not quantitative. Virtually all other schools of economics claim that they can, at least to some extent. But praxeological reasoning quashes intellectual shortcuts. Value judgments and scales are always subjective. Prices aren't facts but expressions of expectations based on individuals' past wants. Economics has little to do with mathematics. They're both a-priori sciences at their core, but each addresses its distinct domain — the subjective and the objective.

"Then I reproached myself with my unthankful temper, and that I had repined at my solitary condition; and now what would I give to be on shore there again! Thus, we never see the true state of our condition till it is illustrated to us by its contraries, nor know how to value what we enjoy, but by the want of it."

– Daniel Defoe, *The Life and Adventures of Robinson Crusoe*

3

RETURNS

Humans need water to survive, and arguably no one needs diamonds. Still, people pay way more for diamonds than water. How can this be? Understanding this phenomenon is crucial to understanding how people value different quantities of goods. The fact that diamonds are more expensive than water can be explained by a phenomenon called *diminishing marginal utility*. The Law of Diminishing Marginal Utility states that all else equal, as consumption increases, the marginal utility derived from each additional unit declines. *Utility* is an economic term that represents satisfaction or happiness. In praxeology, utility represents a person's belief of how well the good or service will help remove a felt uneasiness. In short, an item's utility is determined by how an individual actor values the predicted outcomes of its usage. An item's utility is, therefore, always subjective. A good will typically have a predictable, objective use-value that is distinct from its subjective utility.

For instance, we might objectively conclude that Robinson Crusoe must eat one fish per day to survive. However, Robinson's perceived *utility* from eating a fish is a different matter. A good's utility derives from what an individual actor thinks this good can provide him in terms of serving him as a means to reach his desired ends; how well or efficiently he believes he can alleviate his uneasiness. The utility of a fish to Robinson depends on how satisfactory he *assumes* the act of eating this fish will be. Therefore, the utility of a fish has nothing to do with how much fish Robinson needs to eat to survive. Humans are generally bad at predicting the future, which means we often underestimate or overestimate a good's technical utility (or use-value). To make use of the fish, Robinson must first know how to prepare it. If he doesn't, neither the fish nor its nutritional content will be of any value to him — the fish is useless unless he knows how to utilize it. Thus, a good's potential use value is irrelevant to someone who doesn't know how to utilize that good. Utility, like value, is personal and can only be arranged ordinally, never cardinally.

Now, how do we measure one good against another? By measuring the latest additional unit of one good compared to another without considering the total amount of each. We call this measuring *utility at the margin*. We imagine what utility an additional unit of a good will have before we decide to acquire it as a means to reach our ends. We must always *economize* our means since action implies that these means are scarce. This scarcity leads us to use those means we believe will help us reach our most desired ends first. Thus, every added unit of a homogenous good serves a lesser desirable end than the previous unit. In other words, every additional unit of that good provides a more secondary marginal utility to the acting individual. In this way, the *Law of Diminishing Marginal Utility* helps us make sense of human interactions and trade.

For example, imagine Robinson Crusoe owning three identical half-a-coconut bowls. He uses the first bowl for drinking water, the second for storing utensils, and the third for decoration. Each additional item goes to serve a lesser urgent end. Now imagine that Robinson drops his drinking coconut while pouring water into it one morning, breaking it into two pieces. Will he then stop drinking water altogether because of the incident? Probably not. The decorative bowl will probably replace the drinking bowl since that bowl serves the least urgent end out of the three.

The Law of Diminishing Marginal Utility, which is a fundamental principle of praxeology, does not rely on psychological assumptions or information about the physical objects affected. The law is praxeologically correct precisely because we can use logical deductive reasoning to arrive at it from the axiom of action alone. The action axiom is an irrefutable assumption because arguing against it would require a deliberate effort, which would prove the assumption to be true. Empirical testing of the law would be futile since we can logically prove it true regardless of what the test results would indicate. The Law of Diminishing Marginal Utility tells us that prices are not mechanically set, not even by supply and demand. Individuals' goal-seeking choices determine an item's current market value, and price tags are (mostly) historical data points that tell us what the last buyer of the article was willing to pay. In setting a new price for a good or service, the producer makes a rough estimate of what he thinks the next buyer of the product will be willing to pay.

The means we use to reach our desired ends are called goods. We classify goods into two main categories — consumer goods and producer goods. Consumer goods are those goods that directly satisfy an actor's ends. Producer goods, or *factors of production*, must be combined with at least one other producer good to create a definite quantity of a consumer good. Since this is the case for all producer goods, they only indirectly satisfy an actor's ends. For example, a simple cheese toast is a consumer good. The bread, the cheese, the toaster, and the labor involved in producing the toast are producer goods. Whether an object falls into the former or latter category depends entirely on the individual's end goal. For instance, the bread and the cheese could be consumed directly, independent of the cheese toast. In this case, they would be categorized as consumer goods and not as factors of cheese-toast production.

To find the utility derived from any unit of a homogenous consumer good, one must consider three things:

1. Every human action is an exchange. Action implies preferring one thing over another. Put another way, the cost of choosing one end is determined by whatever other end you could have chosen instead;
2. Action determines value. What one does must logically be what one thought was most urgent; and
3. Preferences, like utility, are arranged ordinally but not cardinally.

Ranking an actor's preferred choices ordinally provides us with a scale revealing that each subsequent end must be less important to the actor since the more urgent want is always satisfied first. Each successive unit of a homogenous consumer good will always aid a lesser pressing urge, as the Law of Diminishing Marginal Utility explains. Calculating this utility arithmetically is impossible because a person's value scale is always ordinal, never cardinal.

Producer goods, also known as factors of production, differ from consumer goods and do not follow the same utility laws. Instead of being consumed and, thereby, satisfying ends instantly, they contribute to the production of consumer goods later down the line. They do not satisfy ends directly. Because they don't, we cannot derive their utility directly, even if the units of the producer good are entirely homogenous. The utility of a producer good, instead, derives from the utility of its marginal product. The *Law of Returns* asserts that for any combination of producer goods, there exists an optimum. Suppose one deviates from this optimum by increasing the input of only one factor of production. In that case, the physical output does not increase — at least not proportionately to the increased production input. Therefore, the Law of Returns is also called the *Law of Diminishing Returns*. All this law tells us is that such an optimum exists, nothing else. The utility of a producer good is its contribution to the end product.

For example, if Robinson aims to build a raft out of driftwood and rope, he will need a certain amount of each good. In this case, the driftwood and the rope serve as producer goods to Robinson. If there's an insufficient amount of driftwood, the raft won't float. Too much driftwood, on the other hand, will make the raft too big and thus harder to maneuver — thus, surplus driftwood is useless to Robinson for this particular end. This situation illustrates that there exists an optimum amount of driftwood for Robinson's specific goal. By "optimal," we mean in the context of serving as a means for Robinson to reach this particular end and nothing else. Note that an extra unit of the other factor of production in the example, more rope, wouldn't add any utility to the raft either. More rope than whatever amount is needed to tie the driftwood together to make a raft will only increase its total weight and make it less seaworthy. Whatever anyone else would think the best way to construct a raft out of these two materials would be, is of no concern to Robinson. To him, all that matters is his assumptions and predictions about the outcome of his actions. Praxeology studies relationships between people and objects, not the objects themselves.

In the case of the diamonds and the water, we can now clearly see that one additional unit of water would be of little value to most people because most people already have access to more water than they need anyway. On the other hand, a diamond is rare and has a high perceived value to many people. Many people thus covet it for its assumed trade value. Still, a person dying of thirst in the Gobi desert would probably be willing to pay more for water than for diamonds, regardless of their rarity.

"All this labor I was at the expense of, purely from my apprehension on the account of the print of a man's foot which I had seen; for as yet I never saw any human creature come near the island, and I had now lived two years under these uneasinesses, which indeed made my life much less comfortable than it was before."

– Daniel Defoe, The Life and Adventures of Robinson Crusoe

4

LABOR

WHENEVER human beings use their physical abilities and skills to produce a good or provide a service, we call it *labor*. In praxeology, labor refers to human energy employed in production. It constitutes another crucial element in production, apart from producer goods. The objects in physical space an actor chooses as means toward a specific end are scarce, and so is human labor. We can release only a limited amount of energy at any given time, so we must always economize our physiological functions. Since we're often aware of how scarce real-world objects are, we also know that we must increase our expenditure of labor to increase production. However, labor does come with its unique limitations.

Whenever a person is not engaged in labor, they're involved in *leisure*. Leisure is, at all times, what action aims toward and always consists of consuming a good or service. This is the praxeological definition of the word "leisure" — a counterpart to labor. Purposeful behavior always aims at the actor's highest valued ends, which they prefer sooner rather than later. Labor involves psychic costs because one must sacrifice leisure to engage in labor. People only participate in physical work because they value the ends that labor will yield more than the cost of forgoing leisure. We always choose between two options — Shall I try to achieve my long-term goals through work, or should I satisfy my ends now? Should I write this book, or should I play computer games? Should I mow the lawn or go to bed? If we can't see any value in the next good or service we'll produce, we will stop working. Leisure is immediately gratifying. Labor is not — when labor's involved, gratification is always delayed. We can enjoy working, but we cannot consume the fruits of our struggle until we stop working and enter leisure mode.

We've established that labor is an element of production. Since leisure is immediately gratifying, we categorize it as a consumer good. When we enjoy leisure, we consume time, often aptly referred to as killing it. Therefore, leisure must also follow the Law of Diminishing Marginal Utility. Under this law, the utility derived from the value of an end created by a certain amount of labor equals the leisure one must sacrifice to engage in that labor. The first unit of leisure will satisfy the most urgent desire, the second unit the second most pressing one, and so on. Therefore, leisure's marginal utility decreases as its supply increases, just as with any other good.

Labor, on the other hand, is all about delayed gratification. Working implies sacrificing immediate gratification for increased gratification later on. We forgo leisure in the present to work towards a goal we believe will bring us higher-valued leisure in the future. Because labor requires sacrificing more immediate ends, it's hard to see the diminishing marginal utility of the end products that labor indirectly produces. Here, it is helpful to introduce the term *disutility of labor*, a phrase that describes the effect labor has on a person's decision to continue working. Just as rationality has nothing to do with sensibility, the disutility of labor has nothing to do with the quality of the work performed. Not in any praxeological sense, that is. The simplest way to think about the disutility of labor is to consider it the flip side of diminishing marginal utility. Each added unit of a consumer good has a diminishing marginal utility, while each extra labor effort has an increasing marginal disutility. In other words, the longer you keep on working, the higher the disutility of your work, at least in terms of your forgone leisure. The value of labor is thus subjective in the same way the value of a consumer good is.

The degree to which people enjoy work varies greatly. Your enjoyment depends on many ever-changing factors. What kind of work you do, how much of it you've done before, how rewarding your goals seem, your personality, and many other factors all contribute to how much you enjoy working. Work is more or less painful, and we experience this pain to varying degrees. In short, we each value the fruits of our labor differently. Knowing all this, we can now logically comprehend the three main limitations in human labor's ability to increase the rate of production over time:

1. The total number of people in existence;
2. The ability of each worker; and
3. How much disutility the work brings to the worker.

We also need to know what time frame we're talking about here. Let's expand on each bullet point.

The total number of people in existence is a necessary first-step factor because labor is a scarce resource. From there, analysis of prongs two and three flow naturally. Like all scarce resources, labor will be ascribed to its most valued ends first. The more people, the higher the labor supply. Therefore, more wants can be satisfied. It is essential to consider each worker's ability because humans are very different from one another, each with varied interests and capabilities. Some people are strong and sturdy, thus suited for physical tasks. Others are nerdy and intelligent, therefore, better at solving theoretical problems. Some are industrious, efficient, and professional. Others work in the public sector. Some are mentally and physically disabled, severely limiting their ability to work efficiently. Also, as explained, how much disutility labor brings to a person is entirely subjective — some value leisure more than others.

At this point, it should be clear that a change in any of these three limitations will lead to a shift in production, assuming all other factors stay constant. It should also be clear that the notion that technological advancements lead to unemployment is wrong. Tools and technologies can never replace labor. All they can do is increase the efficiency of the laborer. As production output increases, the marginal utility for each successive unit of the good produced decreases. This increased output is not a net bad, though — quite the opposite. Technology improvements help us save time and reallocate labor to new, more exciting jobs. If the job market is fair and natural, there's something to do for everyone. The notion that increased labor efficiency could harm people stems from politics, which often paints a skewed picture of societal problems. Unemployment isn't a problem; the real issue is making ends meet, and that's a very individual problem. As we will come to understand, the best way for politicians to enable people to be self-sustainable is to meddle as little as possible with the free market process.

We can now conclude that all human labor has limitations and follows laws derived from the fundamental axioms of praxeology using logic and deductive reasoning alone. These laws are very similar to those that apply to all other scarce means. They tell us that human labor is necessary for the production process of all consumer goods, at least at some level of production. Even a robotic factory requires human labor since someone has to construct the robots and the parts that make them up. People work because they think the end products (their paycheck, for example) are worth the disutility that work brings them. Employers pay employees because of the value they believe the good or service produced will bring them, not because of the hours an employee puts in.

From this praxeological viewpoint, history can be re-analyzed and interpreted. Since we know that all human labor has an attached disutility to each actor, it is no surprise that technological advancements have allowed people to work less now than they did 200 years ago. People are probably happier now than then because more of their wants are satisfied. Technological progress itself is neither good nor bad — but it always saves someone time and capital somewhere. Bad things happen when some individuals try to engineer society itself. Society is a complex web of people acting in their own self-interest, and interfering in this process produces unintended consequences. When people's incentives are tampered with, they will act differently, but not because of some altruistic notion of a greater good. They will change their behavior to what they believe will, more efficiently, satisfy their ends, regardless of what the intent of a particular policy might have been. Therefore, it is impossible to predict what impact even the most negligible tax will have on society in the long run. The dynamic nature of markets renders empirical analysis inadequate and defective. We never get to experience what could have been; thus, it is a fool's errand to rely on empiricism to draw conclusions about the effectiveness of a policy. Because of the unpredictable nature of human action, a-priori reasoning is the only tool we have in our toolbox devoid of opinion, which all scientific claims about human action necessarily have to be. Anything else is opinion at best and propaganda at worst.

After thirteen days on the island and twelve trips to the ship he came from, Robinson Crusoe brought back "about 36 pounds value in money, some European coins, some Brazil, some pieces of eight, some gold and silver." He was amused at the sight of the money because he realized that of all the things he brought off the ship, this money would have the most negligible value for him in his present condition. Robinson exchanged his leisure for labor which turned out to be fruitless. From this moment on in the book, Robinson realizes that the only person he has to trade with on the island is his future self. A commodity's saleability is no longer a concern for him. All he can do from this point on is sacrifice leisure and start working to accumulate capital goods. If he doesn't, nature will force him to catch fish with his bare hands every day. Recognizing what you have — be it physical objects, skills, or connections — and how those things can be useful to your future self is a prerequisite for progress, regardless if you're a castaway or a king.

"In a word, the nature and experience of things dictated to me, upon just reflection, that all the good things of this world are no farther good to us than they are for our use; and that, whatever we may heap up indeed to give others, we enjoy just as much as we can use, and no more."

– Daniel Defoe, *The Life and Adventures of Robinson Crusoe*

5

CAPITAL, TIME AND TRADE

CAPITAL, or time, is the third main element of the three main factors of production. As we've learned, the others are our labor and nature-given means. Praxeologically speaking, capital is essentially the same thing as time. In the same praxeological sense, nature-given means can be called land, and human effort can be called labor. Nature-given means and human labor have limitations in terms of productive output. Therefore, if one wants to increase one's production of consumer goods, one must acquire more time somehow. Time accumulation involves producing and saving goods for consumption in the future. We call this *capital accumulation*, and we call the goods that store time *capital goods*. To understand how humans raise their standard of living, we must first understand the importance of accumulating capital and saving it for future use.

Given what we now know, we can start viewing production in stages, which will ultimately lead to the production of consumer goods. These stages are called the *Structure of Production*. Let's compare a basic production structure to an advanced or complex production structure by once again using a classic hypothetical scenario in praxeology — that of Robinson Crusoe marooned on a tropical island. Robinson's most urgent desire is to feed himself. Luckily, he finds a freshwater lake teeming with fish in the middle of the island. He jumps into the water and starts catching fish with his bare hands. This production structure is almost instantaneous since catching fish with one's hands is only one stage away from eating that same fish. However, the rate at which Robinson can catch fish this way could be faster. When Robinson realizes this, he begins constructing a fishing net. The construction of the net involves several stages of production. First, Robinson must cut down suitable tree branches and separate fibers from them. After that, he must braid those fibers together to form a rope. Finally, he can tie this rope together when he's made enough to create a net. Each step takes a certain amount of time. Jumping into the pond and trying to catch fish by hand takes little time since doing so is a simple, short production structure. But if Robinson wants to increase his rate of production or output, he must first engage in a more complex and, thus, lengthier production structure.

Whether or not Robinson deems constructing the fishing net worthwhile depends solely on his *time preference*. Time preference refers to a person's willingness to give up something in the present for something in the future. Imagine it takes Robinson Crusoe ten working days to build a fishing net. If, during the net's production stages, he dedicates all his waking hours to net production, Robinson won't be able to feed himself. In doing so, he sacrifices immediate satisfaction for a chance to improve his situation in the long run. After constructing the net, Robinson will be able to catch fish faster, giving himself more time to engage in other activities, such as producing even more efficient tools. We call this *delayed gratification* or having a *low time preference*. Whether Robinson ultimately constructs the net depends on whether he finds the increase in his fish-catching rate worth the tradeoff. The same is true for us. A person's time preference can never be zero since no person would wait forever to achieve a specific result, but it can be very low. Some people act almost exclusively on instinct and refuse to accept that having a plan would be better for them in the long run. Others start working on a project at a very young age and don't mind striving for a particular goal all their lives. Time preference is personal and dynamic. We value our time and the well-being of our future selves subjectively, just like everything else in life.

Now how can Robinson Crusoe construct a fishing net without starving to death in the process? There are two ways in which he can solve this problem.

One is to reduce his daily production and consumption of fish, saving a portion of his day for producing a fishing net. The other is to increase his fish output by working longer hours, setting aside any excess fish he can catch for consumption at a later date. The two ways are fundamentally similar and will provide Robinson with the same result. His saved fish represents his *capital*. We call this process *saving*.

At every step, having access to more capital goods puts us closer in time to our enjoyment of consumer goods. Once we realize its importance, we can see that saving is the fundamental action that brings us to higher living standards. The main reason we have such high living standards today is that our ancestors realized the importance of saving and accumulating capital so that they could build the things that make our lives so comfortable today. We no longer have to spend our days hunting for prey, harvesting crops, and looking for shelter. We have freezers, cars, supermarkets, computers, and all sorts of time-saving goods at our disposal, all thanks to the foresight and patience of our ancestors. Like our friend Robinson Crusoe, they all gave up immediate consumption for capital accumulation. All human action is an exchange — either an exchange between you and others or between you and your future self. So far, we've covered interactions between people and their future selves, such as in the example of Robinson Crusoe and his future fishing net. But what if we introduce other people into the mix? For the isolated individual, action always implies forgoing what one could have done for what one actually does. In the case of two or more people interacting, the same principles apply. For a consensual exchange between two people to occur at all, both parties must believe that they will benefit from the deal. In other words, the seller's offered good or service must be higher on the buyer's value scale than whatever good or service he's willing to give up in return for acquiring it. This form of concerted action between two or more individuals to attain definite personal ends can be called a *civilized* interaction. When we voluntarily exchange goods and services, we are being civilized. Hence the word *civilization*.

On the other hand, involuntary interactions between people stand in stark contrast to consensual ones. In these interactions, one of the parties forces the other to give up the good or service using violence or the threat thereof.

We call this way of interacting *uncivilized* or *barbaric*. Transcending barbarism makes societies thrive and flourish because the more civilized a society is, the easier it becomes for its people to achieve their desired goals.

For an exchange between two people to happen, they cannot offer one another the same good or service. If they did, no trade would occur because their respective wants for that particular good would already be satisfied. Therefore, individuals who specialize in producing rare goods and services for the market have a better chance of exchanging them for other things. This results in what we call *division of labor*. The phenomenon of division of labor is a conscious response from individuals who, through reason, recognize the benefits of exchange with their fellow human beings. An excellent example of a well-functioning community where the division of labor makes everyone's life easier is the village depicted in the "Asterix" comic book series. *Getafix* (the druid), *Fulliautomatix* (the smith), *Unhygienix* (the fishmonger), and the series' main protagonists, *Asterix* and *Obelix*, continuously trade goods and services with one another voluntarily within the village's walls. Problems only arise when an aggressor (in most cases, the Romans) tries to confiscate the village's resources using force. We'll analyze the consequences of forceful actions later. For now, let's focus on voluntary interaction and the division of labor.

We're not born equal, regardless of what your teachers might have told you in public school. Life would be pretty dull if we were. There would be no sports since competition would be pointless. No one would ever invent anything since we'd all approach every problem in precisely the same way. Luckily, we're all different and have different skills and talents. If we weren't, evolution wouldn't have taken us very far. We'd probably still be a school of plankton floating around, waiting to be consumed by a whale. The more diverse our capabilities, the more advanced our civilization can become — all thanks to specialization and the division of labor.

Robinson Crusoe might be better than Friday at growing crops, and Friday might be better than Robinson at raising cows. They might also find themselves in different geographical locations where producing one good is more manageable than producing the other. Even the serviceability of the land itself may differ. In this scenario, Robinson is better off growing crops and trading with Friday, and Friday is better off raising cows and trading with Robinson. Because of differences, humans are more productive when they specialize in performing a specific task and exchanging with others rather than trying to do everything themselves. The example of Robinson and Friday might seem obvious, but what's less intuitive is that even if Robinson is better at *both* tasks than Friday, they're better off doing what they're best at and trading with each other than if Robinson was trying to produce it all by himself. Collectively, they are better off exchanging because the total output of goods will be higher if they do so. In other words, if one party is superior to the other at producing all goods, then it should focus on creating the good of which it has the maximum advantage over the other party since this will lead to the best possible outcome for both parties through trade. The author of this text might be better than his wife at washing clothes and writing books about praxeology, but we'll both be better off if I write the book and she washes our clothes. Luckily for me, I'm worse than she is at washing clothes, so the matter isn't even up for debate. The praxeological term for this phenomenon is the *Ricardian Law of Association*, named after the British political economist David Ricardo.

Ricardo demonstrated the consequences of the division of labor when an individual or a group that is more efficient in every respect cooperates with a less efficient one. He concluded that it is advantageous for the superior individual or group to concentrate its efforts upon producing those commodities for which its relative advantage is the highest and to leave the production of other goods to inferior producers. The division of labor between the two increases labor productivity and is advantageous to all concerned, even if one of the individuals or groups is effectively better at producing all goods. It may seem paradoxical that it is more beneficial to specialize and focus on making only one particular thing when you're also better than your competitors at making other things. Remarkably, trading allows even the most disadvantaged to contribute to society through labor division, thereby lifting themselves out of poverty.

On a macro scale, the network of individual voluntary exchanges is what forms a society or civilization. It also creates a pattern of interrelations that we call *the market*. The market creates an opportunity for human beings to engage in production solely for the purpose of trade. We can perform tasks demanded by the market rather than working for ourselves directly and achieve better outcomes for everyone involved. Exchanges occur because of the innate inequalities between people and their nature-given resources. Voluntary exchange and the division of labor push us into more and more specialization. It causes some villages to grow into cities and others to remain farmland. The division of labor playing out for millennia has made us specialize to such a degree that some people now react to reaction videos on the internet for a living. Imagine the stages of production that had to precede such a profession. Every step forward on the road toward a market that satisfies the highest amount of human desires requires more advanced technologies. These advancements, in turn, require a further specialization of tasks.

Contrary to what some politicians assert, the free market benefits everyone, including those who are worse at practically everything than everyone else. The kicker is that this happens regardless of people's motives. Friday may hate Robinson for being superior to him in every conceivable way but still recognize that he is better off trading with him than fighting him. An incentive to voluntarily respect and cooperate with Robinson is inherent since harming him would probably result in a worse net outcome for Friday. By hurting Robinson, Friday would deprive himself of the increased total output that trading with him would have generated. Peaceful interpersonal relationships provide better opportunities for everyone, incentivizing us to become friends through our shared, logically provable values. Praxeology illuminates how deeply we are connected and how rudimentary it is to appreciate other human beings, flawed as they may be. Understanding these concepts and the laws we can derive from them tells us why cooperation and peace are vastly superior to isolation and violence as tools for reaching our individual goals. All you need is love, and probably so.

"Call on me in the day of trouble, and I will deliver, and thou shalt glorify me."

– Daniel Defoe, *The Life and Adventures of Robinson Crusoe*

6

MONEY

So far, we've discussed the direct exchange of goods and services for other things. We've concluded that people trade with themselves and others, and we've stressed the importance of saving for the future. We've also shown how trading benefits everyone, including those with limited productive skills. Your skills are worth more than you might intuitively think. Primarily because of the efficiency acquired through the division of labor, people are better off specializing even when they're better at everything. But what happens when people begin to engage in *indirect* trade via a *medium of exchange*? The most saleable good in society becomes its primary medium of exchange, and we call this commodity *money*. Let's examine what money is and how it works.

In every trade we engage in, we're both buyers and sellers. We sell what's already in our possession to buy what we're trying to obtain. In direct trade or barter, we eventually become aware of two problems — limited *divisibility* of the goods and the necessity for *double coincidence of wants* for those goods. First, what we want to sell might not be divisible enough to match what we intend to buy, and vice versa. Second, the person we want to trade with might not be interested in whatever good or service we offer them. These two problems drastically curtail both parties' ability to reach their desired ends by limiting their trading options.

Imagine a rabbit-catching Robinson and a fish-catching Friday. Friday is willing to trade four fish for one rabbit. His challenge is to find a rabbit hunter (like Robinson), not in need of just some fish but of the exact quantity that Friday is willing to give up. In other words, Friday's and Robinson's wants need to coincide for any exchange to take place. The other problem with barter trade is that most goods aren't divisible enough to be suitable as media of exchange. Imagine, for instance, that Friday wanted to trade one fish for one-fourth of a rabbit. Which parts of a rabbit are worth what? A rabbit is relatively *indivisible*. In a barter economy, people produce fewer goods that are hard to divide because they are problematic to sell. Tools and machinery are often challenging to divide into smaller parts. The divisibility problem plays a massive role in why barter economies can't become as advanced as societies that use a good form of money. Without a functioning universal medium of exchange, human society is doomed to stay in a primitive state.

The problems of indivisibility and the necessity for coinciding wants can only be solved using an indirect media of exchange. Indirect exchange means the buyer acquires a good intended solely for trade before the interaction occurs. Some goods are more useful as media of exchange and therefore become more valuable to market actors for this specific purpose. These goods are neither designed for production nor consumption but for the sole purpose of facilitating transactions. Because of their usefulness as media of exchange, these goods emerge in the market as *monetary goods*. A good's usefulness as a facilitator of indirect exchange is called its *saleability*, in other words, how easy the good is to sell. The good with the highest saleability becomes what we commonly refer to as *money*. A snowball effect ensues once this monetary good emerges in the market, and people begin saving it for later use in trade. Praxeology is not concerned with which commodity the market prefers as money. What praxeology does study is the implications of the emergence of money on that market's actors.

All sorts of goods have been used as money throughout history. Gold, silver, copper, salt, peppercorns, tea, decorated belts, shells, alcohol, cigarettes, silk, candy, nails, cocoa beans, cowries, and barley have all had their time in the spotlight. Their natural qualities have contributed to their long-term use as money. But one particular commodity has stood the test of time better than the others — gold. Gold incorporates all six fundamental characteristics of money — *durability, portability, divisibility, uniformity, limited supply, and acceptability*. A good form of money must be durable to store its value over time. It must be portable to facilitate trade over large distances — if it's too heavy, it becomes difficult to carry around. As discussed earlier, good money also needs to be divisible. Lack of divisibility is one of the two fundamental problems money needs to solve. The monetary units must also be uniform to enable *economic calculation*. More on this later. Their supply needs to be limited too. Otherwise, inflation will run amok and dilute the monetary value of the good. Finally, money must be broadly accepted. But acceptance is just another word for saleability, and goods become highly saleable if they fit the other five criteria for becoming money. The only thing that could limit a good or commodity's saleability would be a prohibition of using it in trade. When people no longer have to care about divisibility and the double coincidence of wants, the division of labor begins to function better by orders of magnitude. As everyone can now trade their goods and services for money, civilizational advancements can materialize much faster, and technologies can become vastly more sophisticated. Money can be spent on capital- or consumer goods, allowing for shorter routes to achieving one's ends, regardless of how hard it would be to achieve those ends by working in solitude. No one on Earth can construct a computer by themselves. In fact, it is impossible for a single person to produce something as trivial as a pencil on their own. The wood, the compressed graphite in the center, the brass ferrule, the glue that holds it together, the yellow paint, and the color for the black lines are all produced separately and exchanged for money. Most likely, a barter economy wouldn't even spawn the saw that cut down the tree for the wood! Money makes civilization possible, and a functioning monetary system is as vital to society as the cardiovascular system is to the human body.

People express subjective value judgments through a common denominator using money. We call these expressions *prices*. To understand the importance of prices and price signals, we must first understand how people engaging in direct exchange determine prices. Prices express exchange rates between two goods. Suppose Friday exchanges four fish for one of Robinson's rabbits. Then the price of one rabbit would be four, denominated in fresh fish. Conversely, the price of a fish denominated in rabbits is one-fourth of a rabbit. Which fourth is still debatable, though.

It is also important to remember that prices are primarily historical data points. They tell us nothing about how people will assess the future value of their respective goods. Because prices are historical exchange ratios between two goods or services, one of them being money, a price tag represents what someone was willing to pay for a good or service at a specific time. When a trade occurs, the transaction price reveals that at some point in time, the seller valued X amount of the good they were buying, usually money, higher than the good they were selling and that the inverse was true for the buyer. Prices can also represent what the buyer wants for the good, but not necessarily what they can get. The only thing differentiating money from all other goods is that money can also serve as a common denominator for all other goods and services on the market. A common denominator unlocks the ability to perform economic calculations for the actor. The number of units of money you possess gives you a rough estimate of your ability to acquire goods and services quickly. It is only possible to perform this calculation when you know the prices of the various goods and services available to you. These economic calculations allow market actors to analyze their successes and failures. They can tell you how close you are to achieving your goals in terms of a specific good in your possession — money.

If a loaf of bread costs one unit of money and a bottle of milk costs four units, we can quickly derive that a bottle of milk is worth four loaves of bread on the market. Calculating allows us to keep *balance sheets*. We can evaluate and estimate how much yield our current stock of goods will bring us using our knowledge of day-to-day prices. This knowledge helps us become more economically efficient. It also helps us avoid wasting resources since it can prevent us from overproducing stuff people don't want or need. Put another way — good money prevents *malinvestment*. It is important to remember that money is *not* a measurement of value but rather a value-signaling tool. One cannot measure value objectively, and praxeology recognizes this. As explained earlier, the subjective nature of value is one of the fundamental pillars of praxeology. Arguments against the subjective nature of value judgments are value judgments themselves. They express how the person values the validity of the claim that value is subjective, thereby proving the thesis correct. The natural sciences deal in absolutes. They can model reality, but the accuracy of these models depends on whatever input variables we select. Correspondingly, the output is dependent on the input. Despite all this, the numerical calculations engineers use when constructing bridges and skyscrapers are usually very reliable. These equations have stood the test of time and continue to provide us with many tools for understanding the nature of objective reality. But we cannot apply the numerical calculations of engineers and physicists to economics. Thus, neither can we rely on empirical evidence since the market and the wants and needs of its participants are ever-changing and dynamic.

Regarding the subjective concept of value, we lack a universal way to generate mathematical models for whatever we're trying to figure out. Mathematics can provide the engineer with the tools he needs to construct a bridge to be strong enough to support the cars that will eventually cross it. But it cannot tell him anything about whether or not building the bridge was worth the effort in the first place. Only economic calculation can give us a clue as to whether building the bridge was a good idea or not. Financial analysis and economic calculation can tell the bridge maker if constructing the bridge would strip another, more urgent project of the material factors and labor needed to satisfy a more urgent need. In other words, the only way an engineer can estimate the *opportunity cost* of not building the bridge is through economic calculation using money prices. For example, the engineer could allocate the capital goods and labor needed to make the bridge to drilling a tunnel instead. An engineer can use steel and concrete for many purposes, but only price signals tell him what to do with these resources. Money transmits information through prices and tells entrepreneurs where to focus and which means to use.

Entrepreneurs always search for the most profitable allocation of their time and resources — the best and most efficient use of resources to satisfy other people's most vital and urgent desires. *Profit*, monetary or otherwise, is always a desirable end for market actors. Both buyers and sellers seek to maximize profit, turning the whole economic apparatus in everyone's favor. Profit is always good, regardless of what proponents of various political movements may profess. Some political opinions stem from a misunderstanding of what constitutes profit. Profit, per se, is not the same as monetary gains. Discovery through economic calculation is limited and does not apply to things that can't be bought and sold for money. Love, happiness, self-esteem, and artistic expression are examples of things outside the realm of economic calculation. These play a societal role, but we cannot categorize them as economic activity. These things, around which we cannot calculate using prices, are either ends in themselves or non-exchangeable consumer goods. No economic calculation is necessary (or even able) to determine their value by an acting human being. When Charles Kane, the protagonist of the classic movie *Citizen Kane*, is on his deathbed, he keeps repeating the word "Rosebud." The meaning of the word remains shrouded in mystery for most of the film until it is eventually revealed to be the name of Kane's beloved sled from his childhood. Kane has a traumatic memory of the sled being burnt to ashes, implying that his motivations throughout the movie stem more from his childhood trauma than pure economic reasoning.

To further illustrate the subjective nature of valuation and profit, imagine (far-fetched pun intended) that Paul Mc Cartney and Ringo Starr get an offer of one billion dollars to re-unite The Beatles without John and George. The money offered may seem very tempting, but they take pride in their legacy as a whole group. One cannot express pride in money terms. They now have to choose whether giving up their pride for a billion dollars is worth it. If they decide to take the offer, they will lose a lot of fans who will deem them greedy. Some fans may even blame Paul and Ringo's selfish behavior on capitalism. Can a pile of cash make people selfish in this way? Of course not. The existence of money merely makes the moral decision easier for Paul and Ringo since it makes economic calculation easier. If someone had offered each of them a golden Lamborghini, they would have been confronted with the same moral dilemma, but it would have been more challenging for them to weigh one choice over the other. Regardless, it is the offer itself that presents them with the ethical dilemma, not the unit of account in which it is denominated. Money prices merely communicate information about things bought and sold against it — nothing more, and more importantly, nothing less.

In a functioning society, people evaluate their potential actions based on expected costs, revenues, and past efforts with profit and loss accounting. Since the discovery of money, these calculations have been much easier to perform, dramatically increasing the supply of material goods on the global market. Therefore, humans have more time for leisure and consuming non-exchangeable goods than ever before. At least, that would have been the case if we weren't living in the last stages of the fiat currency paradigm, but that's a whole different discussion.

"Being the third son of the family and not bred to any trade, my head began to be filled very early with rambling thoughts."

– Daniel Defoe, The Life and Adventures of Robinson Crusoe

7

MARKETS

WHETHER you like it or not, you're a capitalist if you own capital goods. Proper economic calculation is only possible after the introduction of money in the free market. Most people own some capital goods, and money best serves the owners of such goods. Capitalism is merely another word for a system in which people get to keep their capital goods and do with them as they please. Put differently — it is the system that naturally emerges in human society when theft and other violent interventions aren't hindering the process. When actors trade with one another for mutual benefit, a pattern emerges. We call this pattern the market. The praxeological term for studying market phenomena is called *catallactics*. It differs from what we commonly refer to as economics in that the study of catallactics considers all aspects of human action, not just those actions that deal with monetary exchanges, as is the case with traditional economics. Catallactics is more thorough because human action isn't limited to material, exchangeable goods. No good is ever valued based solely on its intrinsic properties.

There is, in fact, no such thing as *intrinsic value*.

We're always willing to pay more for a good or service if we think it will satisfy our most urgent desires more quickly, regardless of what those desires may be. People are generally willing to pay more for food served in a restaurant than the food they must prepare themselves. A home with a stunning view in an international metropolis is typically worth more than one in a dull, one-horse town in the middle of nowhere. The only way to thoroughly explain such phenomena is by taking the subjective opinions of individual humans into account. Catallactics leaves no room for error by recognizing that humans make individual decisions that vary from person to person and from situation to situation.

Words, and their precise definitions, are essential to praxeology. When we say that a buyer always tries to buy at the lowest price possible and that a seller always tries to sell at the highest price possible, it is of utmost importance to remember what we mean by price. In this case, price means something very personal. The buyer always tries to buy at the lowest price possible to them. This lowest price doesn't necessarily have to be the lowest money price for the good, but the lowest price for them to satisfy their most urgent desires. For example, a person can choose to pay more dollars or euros for a good or service if he buys it from a friend since he values this friendship more than the money he could have saved by purchasing the same thing for a few bucks less. Indeed, individuals always aim at maximizing profits, but only if the word includes earnings in terms of non-exchangeable goods as well as exchangeable ones. Economic theories that omit non-exchangeable goods from the equation are not rooted in reality. The financial models central planners and market analysts use to predict markets can break at any point precisely because they refuse to consider individual human beings' ever-changing wants and desires.

Since praxeology is an a-priori science, it does not study human behavior empirically. The a-priori approach, or the *Austrian Method*, compels praxeologists to always arrive at their conclusions using reason alone. The notion that people always act to maximize profits in monetary terms is an imaginary construction, albeit not a very useful one when trying to understand human behavior in markets. Traditional economists make predictions based on this incomplete understanding of why people do things. Praxeologists also use imaginary constructions, but only to single out the elements of reality they aim to study. The "Robinson Crusoe and his fishing pond" —scenario exemplifies one such imaginary construction. Praxeological reasoning involves imagining scenarios where one or more market elements are absent and using these scenarios to analyze the consequences of these elements' presence. Arguments for intervention in the free market, such as the introduction of minimum wage laws, fail to assess how individual market actors will adapt to the altered state of the now not-so-free market to which the intervention will inevitably lead. Free market interferences always bring unintended consequences in their wake.

The Broken Window Fallacy, first explained by the 19th-century French economist Frederic Bastiat in his 1850 essay *That Which We See and That Which We Do Not See*, perfectly illustrates the perils of ignoring the inevitable second-order consequences of market interventions. In Bastiat's tale, a boy breaks one of his father's windows, triggering a chain reaction of inaccurate conclusions. The townspeople (and a horde of confused "modern economists") falsely conclude that the boy has contributed to the overall economy since his father will now have to replace the window and pay the town's glazier to replace the broken pane. The glazier will then spend the extra money on something else, which they believe will stimulate the economy. What they fail to see is the bigger picture. The boy's father is forced to forgo some other good or service he could have procured because of his more acute problem. He must pay the glazier to repair the broken window before he can satisfy some lesser urgent desire.

Moreover, the producer of whatever good or service the father might have bought is now deprived of a customer. The window-breaking also forces the father and the glazier to spend their time and capital re-building a capital good already used in the town's economy, namely, the window. The window was already providing the family with the service of sheltering them. Catallactics is the branch of praxeology that studies the roots, ramifications, and consequences of all interactions on the market. To understand the effects of involuntary market interventions, we must first understand what drives individual human action. After comprehending individual action, we must learn how voluntary exchanges work in an unhampered free market. Only then can we begin to analyze what happens when we introduce other factors, such as interventions, to the equation. The free market has no designer or centralized authority making decisions for it. It is not a place or a group of people doing specific things. The free market is the process that stems from voluntary exchanges between people in absolute control of their property. Those who possess their property can direct it to wherever they believe it to be most beneficial for them to reach their desired goals. They also help others get closer to their personal goals by trading with them. From this perspective, an individual is both a means and an end. A human being is a means for other people to satisfy their ends and an end to herself because she acts to fulfill her personal goals.

Money allows people to determine how others value their offers using a common denominator. As explained earlier, when two people exchange goods, a price arises. The price is nothing but the exchange ratio between the two things. Through the process of trade, a medium of exchange quickly emerges. We call this medium money. Money provides society with prices. Prices inform producers about what to produce, how and where to produce it, and in what quantity. Almost every human being counts as a producer. All people who construct or buy capital goods are producers. They choose to forgo the consumption of goods in the present to be able to consume more in the future. They decide to save rather than spend and delay their immediate gratification for what they believe can bring them more satisfaction later. Anyone engaged in saving for the future is, by definition, also a capitalist. The following statement may surprise you, but we are all capitalists, consumers, laborers, entrepreneurs, and producers. In praxeology, these terms refer to different modes of action — not to people's personality types or a person's social class. A person acts as a capitalist when saving, a consumer when spending, a laborer when forgoing leisure for work, an entrepreneur when setting up a business and taking on financial risks in the hope of profit, and a producer when buying or constructing capital goods. Money allows people to think in terms of accounting, which enables them to evaluate their current financial situation and use this information to determine a suitable path forward to fulfill their desires.

Accounting allows people to differentiate between their capital and their income. Income is whatever amount of money a person can use within a specific period without sacrificing a part of their capital or capital goods. Spending your capital on consumer goods is stealing from your future self in this sense. The distinction between capital and income allows people to live within their means — an expression that, praxeologically speaking, means precisely that. Economic calculation always involves determining one's income, savings, and capital consumption levels.

Blaming free-market capitalism for societal problems is like blaming biology for the existence of hunger. What would increase Robinson's and Friday's chances of survival on the island more — fighting one another or cooperating with one another? Capitalism is a potent way for humans to acquire their ends through fewer means by interacting voluntarily with each other. Any attempt at solving societal problems that hinder the market process reduces its functionality, which is detrimental to everyone involved. In the free market, all participants communicate the consequences of their chosen actions when purchasing goods and services, e.g., withholding from buying a good or service signals to producers that they need to lower their prices or produce better goods. When producers fail to satisfy the needs of their customers, they suffer losses. The consumers will choose another producer's goods and services instead, rewarding producers who best meet their customers' needs.

In stark contrast to what happens to entrepreneurs who fail to meet their customers' needs on the free market, politicians and bureaucrats have a much more comfortable relationship with consequences. We all suffer the repercussions when bureaucrats or politicians make mistakes. A politician who makes terrible decisions may lose the next election — but we cannot know whether getting re-elected was the politician's original intent. Chances are that getting elected into office was merely a means for them to reach another, more urgent, personal end.

If we compare votes cast in a democracy to free-market actions, we notice some crucial differences. In a democracy, only a majority of people, who all need to compromise their beliefs to some extent, get to decide policies. In the free market, every purchase is a vote, and every participant is at least indirectly involved in every decision since every action impacts the market as a whole. The richer you are, the more "votes" you're allowed to cast, and in a free market, financial success is equivalent to helping others fulfill their wants and needs.

When discussing these matters, it is crucial to remember that a completely free market economy has never existed. What humanity has experienced so far has not even been close to it. Interventions in the market and manipulations of the money supply have been around for as long as anyone can remember, and the societies we live in today are no different. It is unlikely that anyone alive today will live long enough to experience a free global market without corruption, taxes, and a manipulated money supply. But to fully grasp what these interventions do to society, we must first understand the imaginary construct of a completely free market.

In the imaginary construction of a completely free market, no group or class decides what other people should or should not do. Each individual is sovereign and freely chooses how to use their property. In their struggle to achieve satisfaction, they can use the guidance of all other market participants' actions expressed through price signals. The market is an evolutionary process, and whatever state it is in is the outcome of people's attempts to adjust their actions in the best possible way to survive and thrive in the world into which they were born. Economic calculation is only possible using money and price signals. Praxeology focuses on pure market interactions because they are the only modes of human action to which we can apply calculations. Before money, economics was not a science at all. And until the discovery of praxeology, economists studied money as an isolated phenomenon and could only partially comprehend or grasp the true power of a free market economy. The outdated ideas of these proto-economists sadly live on today, hindering humanity's civilizational advancement.

Outdated macroeconomic models and flawed ideas about money influence decision-makers and political leaders all over the globe to this day, leading them to adopt self-destructive policies. Likewise, superstition and religious fantasies still influence large groups of people and their decisions, even though the natural sciences and peer-reviewed, a-posteriori empiricism have proven most of these ancient theories wrong. Only through a-priori reasoning and first principles thinking can the flawed arguments of proto-economists be proven wrong once and for all. Praxeology reveals that all self-proclaimed emperors are naked—all humans act for the same fundamental reason. They want to remove themselves from a state of felt uneasiness. Only in this sense are we all truly equal.

"But as abused prosperity is oftentimes made the very means of our greatest adversity, so it was with me."

– Daniel Defoe, *The Life and Adventures of Robinson Crusoe*

8

COMPETITION

IN THE imaginary construct of the completely free market, there are no slaves or masters. Competition exists, but free-market competition is different from other types of competition, like sports. In the market, sellers compete by offering buyers the lowest possible prices. But buyers compete too. They try to accumulate money to afford the highest possible prices. In the imaginary perfect free market, there is no violence. Every person's most substantial incentive is to help others achieve their goals simply because this is the best way they can serve themselves. This type of competition has no losers. Collaborative competition is a civilized way of fighting over scarce resources, which is not to be confused with the uncivilized, violent competition of outright war over these same resources — the type of competition that often occurs between animals.

We will, from now on, differentiate between the two by introducing the terms *biological competition* and *catallactic competition*. Catallactic competition eliminates the need for bloodshed so society can assemble a cooperative pecking order instead of a winner-takes-all scheme. Those who fail in the market end up with fewer options, but as long as they can provide others with value, they're still in it, albeit in a more modest position in the overarching social hierarchy. Therefore, catallactic competition is the most sincere form of collaboration there is.

The concept of freedom is only relevant when referring to human relations.

When an individual has the power to rule another through violent means or threats, the latter is not free. In other words, only in a free market are people genuinely free. Whether Robinson Crusoe is free or not when he's all alone on the island is of no concern to praxeology. An isolated individual is always free to do what he wants. To live free among other people, however, must mean that one can interact with them in non-violent ways without imposed restrictions. A restriction of personal freedom is a violent act in itself. Whoever sets the parameters of constraint limits the options of those affected by it through threats of violence. For example, governments will throw you in jail if you don't pay your taxes.

There can be no compulsion or coercion in a free society. In a free society, people can use their bodies and property however they please as long as their actions don't infringe on other people's property or freedom. Freedom and property are two sides of the same coin. Without absolute property rights, freedom is limited. Therefore, the praxeological definition of freedom becomes "The sphere in which an individual is in a position to choose between alternative modes of action."

The flip side of the freedom coin is responsibility. Only when you are ready to take absolute responsibility for your actions can you consider yourself free. Responsibility separates childhood from adulthood; by this definition, the vast majority of the Earth's population can not be defined as adults today. Personal responsibility causes people to enter adulthood faster, granting them greater freedoms later in life. In a free market system without enforced social security programs, everyone is held accountable for their actions by themselves as well as by their peers. The lion at the zoo may enjoy free housing and food every day but would stand little chance in a fight against a lion that has managed to thrive in the fierce battlefield of the savannah. The caged animal is in the clutches of her captor, as is the recipient of government subsidies and grants. Fortunately for humans, we can claw back our freedoms by taking responsibility for our lives and acting that out in the market. Whenever we offer a good or service on the market, we simultaneously attempt to emancipate ourselves from some of our financial burdens.

In a free society, the limitations to a person's freedom are the laws of nature and the boundaries of praxeology alone. An individual is thus free to the extent that he can choose ends and the means used to attain those ends. One can not attain incompatible ends. Suppose a man wants to jump out of an airplane. The laws of nature stop him from surviving the jump unless he has a parachute. To acquire a parachute, he must attain the means to reach this desired end. The most efficient way for him to acquire a parachute is to sell his services on the market, accumulate capital, and purchase the parachute when he can afford it. He can also steal the parachute, but in doing so, he is no longer a part of civilized society but acting against his own and everyone else's long-term interests.

By stealing from the parachute merchant, the eager para-jumper ends up stealing from himself because he is tampering with the free market process, reducing the long-term benefits of the division of labor. If everyone chose to steal everything, there would soon be nothing left to steal. Stealing from others is stealing from one's future self. In a civilized society, no one is free to violate another's freedom. Any argument against this insight is contradictory because imposing one's will on another person is, de facto, not civilized. Will-imposing behavior belongs not to the catallactic competition underpinning the free market but to the category of biological competition. To be civilized is to be peaceful when interacting with others.

People are not born equal. Everyone has a different set of abilities and personality traits. Physical and mental capacity also varies widely from person to person. Furthermore, people value ends differently. Whether a society's wealth- and income gaps are big or small is not a praxeological concern. Praxeology can tell us how peaceful rather than forceful interactions always produce a better net outcome for everyone involved. But praxeology does not make value judgments based on these outcomes. If it did, it would be as biased as any other so-called "social science." It is not the job of science to suggest what to do about a perceived problem. A proper science describes reality as it is, not what it ought to be according to anyone's opinion. What praxeology *can* do is analyze what role inequality plays in human action.

Human action is always born out of individual dissatisfaction. Market competition arises from a seller's inability to satisfy his customers' wants and needs. It is precisely this inequality between what sellers have to offer that makes everyone try to be better than their competitors in the market. Everyone does their best to satisfy their customers in every market stage because this is the most efficient way to meet their personal goals. The better they satisfy the wants and needs of other people, the more means they acquire, which they can use to benefit themselves. Even though some are born with inherent disabilities, everyone is still better off focusing on what they do best.

If Robinson is better than Friday at catching rabbits and Friday is better at catching fish, they will both be better off if they specialize in what they do best and trade what they produce. In fact, even if Robinson is better at rabbit hunting and fish catching, they're still better off focusing on whatever they do best, as explained by the *Ricardian law of Association* — a collaboration between the more talented and the less gifted always benefits both. The gains derived from the division of labor are thus always mutual.

Importantly, as the division of labor is allowed to produce its magic, more capital becomes available to "help the needy," which everyone is entitled to do to any extent they wish. The freer the market, the more room there is for charity and altruism. On the other hand, if a society allows a central authority to redistribute wealth among its citizens, a plethora of unintended consequences come into play. First, the net amount of resources available for redistribution will decrease over time because a centrally managed market inherently confiscates capital. Secondly, the only way for a centralized entity to acquire wealth for redistribution is to take it from those who've peacefully accumulated it by providing others with satisfactory products and services. By doing so, the centralized authority incentivizes unproductivity and disincentivizes productivity. In light of this undeniable fact, it is easy to see how involuntary redistribution is detrimental to society. To add sour icing to the already rotten cake, all confiscation of wealth makes economic calculation harder for both the victim and the recipient, especially if done regularly and the rules are ever-changing, which is nearly always the case when politicians are involved. When you deliberately make economic calculation harder, you force people to adopt a higher time preference, leading to more short-term decisions and an even more handicapped market process.

Before understanding human behavior in general and violent behavior in particular, one must accept that all democratic governments are inherently violent. The market process is incompatible with all forms of forced government because a world where every interaction is consensual is devoid of compulsion or coercion. Government implies violence, always. Violence is antithetical to free market capitalism and reduces people's power to organize themselves through peaceful cooperation. If a government is allowed to exist, people can never be equal regarding their rights. They can have similar rights to every other serf or slave but never the same rights as the ruling class. For a human right to be ethical, it must be equally valid to every human being alive. Therefore, there can be only one universal human right — the right to be left alone.

The inequalities of wealth, ability, talent, and income among people are all essential for the free market to function. Freedom and order arise from people's efforts to reach their ends through non-violent means. The market is not a survival-of-the-fittest, winner-takes-all, law-of-the-jungle type of competitive environment, regardless of what mainstream media government mouthpieces might insist. The free market is more akin to an antidote for such poisonous modes of conduct. Only by recognizing that the best way of helping yourself is to help others (and vice versa) can we debunk the propaganda and elevate ourselves to become more civilized to one another. When we do, we all win.

Note that one can arrive at these conclusions without having any opinion on what people ought or ought not to do. These are logical conclusions stemming from arguments one cannot dispute without falling into the trap of self-contradiction. Argumentation is a form of human action — using linguistic means to acquire a desired end, namely changing another person's opinion or understanding of a subject. One cannot argue against this proposition without contradicting oneself either. But one can make another person change their mind about practically any matter by forcing them to do so using threats of violence. Making the distinction between what constitutes a non-violent act and a violent one is paramount for understanding why there's often a dissonance between what people say and what they do. Lying about our true intentions is something we do when we feel compelled to do so to reach goals that rank higher on our value scale than being honest.

People who value getting into positions of power above everything else have no problem lying since their desired end dwarfs all other goals they may have, including being an honest person. Depressingly enough, this willingness to sacrifice integrity often helps them reach this goal. On the other hand, leaders with something to lose from not meeting what people expect of them — those with *skin in the game* — are likelier to be telling the truth about their intentions. In reality, catallactic and biological competitions intertwine, and people use various means to reach their goals, some honest and peaceful, others less so. To fully understand how these means affect society, we must clearly distinguish which falls into what category.

"He told me it was men of desperate fortunes on one hand, or of aspiring, superior fortunes on the other, who went abroad upon adventures, to rise by enterprise, and make themselves famous in undertakings of a nature out of the common road."

– Daniel Defoe, *The Life and Adventures of Robinson Crusoe*

9

ENTREPRENEURSHIP

ALL HUMAN ACTION is the conscious aim of an individual to satisfy a particular desire. Always with the ultimate goal of relieving a felt uneasiness. Any desire the person fulfills counts as being of profit to that individual. Any personal desire the actor fails to meet is called a loss. Gains and losses, like all other value judgments, are entirely subjective because they include non-exchangeable goods as well as exchangeable ones. Thus, we can define profit as the satisfaction attained minus the satisfaction forgone. Therefore, all human action seeks profit.

Even suicide is a profit-seeking action. A person engaged in self-murder seeks profit since they value the presumed comfort of death more than the apparent discomfort of life. Even actions directly aimed at helping other people are profitable to the actor. Altruists giving away their wealth to charity are also profit seekers. They hold the warm, fuzzy feeling of being friendly to their fellow humans in higher regard than whatever else they could do with their capital. In this sense, all actions are selfish because they aim to remove or decrease the uneasiness the actor apparently feels. One cannot claim to be "against profits" without simultaneously being "for losses." Praxeology aims at understanding the consequences of various modes of action but never judges the motives behind the action. Science does not adjudicate whether an effort is fair or unfair but rather reveals that all human effort aims toward personal profit. Searching for profit and avoiding losses is, essentially, all we do.

Material profits and losses are different from psychological profits and losses. When people use the terms profit and loss, they typically refer to the material aspect — monetary profit and loss. The success or failure of actions in the market translates into profits and losses that are measurable in monetary terms. In the market, profit means a surplus of money after a set of exchanges, and loss means a shortage. The more profit an entrepreneur enjoys in a completely free market, the better he has satisfied his consumers' needs.

Since markets are predicated on human behavior, they always contain uncertainty. The better an entrepreneur anticipates how to meet his customers' wants and needs in the most efficient way possible amidst this uncertainty, the higher his profit will be. Failed predictions lead to losses. An entrepreneur's profit level tells him how well he satisfied his customers' desires during the interval he measured that profit. The greater the divide between what customers are willing to pay and the cost of all factors that went into production, the more profitable the venture becomes. Therefore, the entrepreneur always has the incentive to reduce production costs. In doing so, he instills a pricing competition between himself and all other entrepreneurs. This profit-seeking competition is what drives consumer prices down. However, prices tell us nothing about the satisfaction of the seller or the buyer at any given moment. Instead, prices signal to entrepreneurs how well they serve their clients. The clients express their opinions about the producer's performance through their actions — if the price is too high, they won't buy the product. If they buy the product, they signal to the entrepreneur that they value that product more than that sum of money at that time. In doing so, they provide the entrepreneur with a method for optimizing the price tag of that product.

All human action is speculation, but the catallactic term *entrepreneurship* refers to determining how to allocate capital goods for particular commercial purposes in the best possible way. Entrepreneurship is risking one's capital to make a profit. Contrast this with capital, which is the act of accumulating capital goods for later use. In the market, all entrepreneurs, whether acting as individuals or on behalf of an organization, are capitalists. To make a profit, they must put capital at risk and serve customers better than their competitors. The CEO of a large corporation gets to decide how to make the best use of its capital. The CEO may look at wages worldwide, move the corporation's production facilities to a low-income area, and then ship the product to where people are willing to pay the highest price possible. Price discrepancies between places provide the entrepreneur with an opportunity. Other entrepreneurs then take note of the first mover's success, whereby they can make similar moves to increase their profits, increasing market competition and lowering consumer prices in the process.

From the consumer's perspective, falling prices are way more important than increased wages since falling prices help everyone while simultaneously increasing the efficiency of the market process. Redistribution schemes only temporarily alleviate the subsidy recipients' financial burdens while simultaneously reducing the market process's efficiency. Furthermore, the first company's profits will decrease as more competitors enter the market. This competition reduces the first company's chances of becoming a monopoly. Unsurprisingly, large corporations often lobby for increased regulatory policies for this very reason. The more they can reduce market competition, the longer they can profit from their monopoly position. Government officials and giant international corporations are thus incentivized to help one another at the expense of everyone else. And their incentives grow stronger the more interdependent they become. The only way to break this vicious cycle would be to introduce, onto the free market, something they can't regulate. But that's a whole different discussion. For now — let's focus on principled, honest entrepreneurship.

If becoming a successful entrepreneur is the most efficient way for a person to contribute to the betterment of society, why aren't we taught entrepreneurship in school? The answer is surprisingly simple — entrepreneurship is not a skill that can be taught. All profitable entrepreneurial endeavors have one thing in common — they add something new to the market. Something novel that no one else is thinking about at the moment. Whether this is a new product, production method, or way to allocate capital goods doesn't matter. Entrepreneurs pursue undiscovered discrepancies between prices and consumer needs. Their success is always linked to their ability to see what others can't. The entrepreneurs' level of formal education might help them connect the dots, but entrepreneurship is more of a mindset than a skill one can teach to others. Entrepreneurship is a creative endeavor interwoven with personal risk-taking. Capital is a prerequisite for progress. Formal education is not. Education can only provide students with theories and tutorials already developed by society. Schools and universities can teach people how to become functioning cogs in the existing societal machine but never how to improve the machine itself. To become an entrepreneur, one must see something others don't and put capital at risk to fill a gap in the market. In this sense, successful entrepreneurial endeavors are the market's equivalent of scientific breakthroughs.

As previously discussed, a person can simultaneously fulfill the roles of the wage earner and the entrepreneur. Entrepreneurs don't earn wages. Instead, they make money through profits. However, all wage earners are simultaneously entrepreneurs since all people allocate capital goods in some way, shape, or form to acquire profits. Entrepreneurial endeavors can make a person more money than wage earning can, but only because the entrepreneur is willing to take on greater risk and accept uncertainty in their future cash flows. A worker takes on a lower risk by trading away the ability to make more money for the certainty of a regular wage check. In some cases, this can allow the worker to become an entrepreneur in his spare time since the regularity of the payouts might make him dare to embark on an entrepreneurial venture he otherwise wouldn't have. In choosing our actions, we must all balance certainty and risk in our lives and consider both when deciding how to spend our days.

If Friday agrees to help Robinson catch fish for x hours per day for one rabbit per day, he trades away x hours per day for the certainty of a daily rabbit meal. This certainty is valuable to Friday because it relieves him of the need to find food every day. He has removed some uncertainty about his future by accepting a steady job and paycheck. The sense of security a steady paycheck brings may or may not enable a person to launch entrepreneurial ventures on their own. Another example would be a certain author of books on praxeology who happened to have a steady day job when he first embarked on his writing journey and started selling books and giving lectures in his spare time.

It is important to remember that profits and losses are two sides of the same coin. When entrepreneurs make huge profits, they signal to the market that some projects are squandering resources and that there are many opportunities for those who want to fix the problems. Losses give the opposite signal. They signal to the market that a particular entrepreneur is wasting resources and that copying their behavior is probably not a good idea. Regardless, the imaginative entrepreneur always has an array of opportunities as long as the market is allowed to function in a natural way. As soon as someone starts tampering with the market process, the price signal gets distorted, and the noise from this distortion makes it harder to see these opportunities.

Capitalism cannot work its magic if society punishes profit makers, nor can the market function properly if society collectivizes losses. The only way for a civilization to progress is to let these phenomena play out in a way that genuinely reflects how well the entrepreneurs satisfy the wants and needs of the consumers. When a society tampers with the free market incentive structure, it reduces that market's functionality. The market is the best tool humans have for punishing resource-wasteful behavior and rewarding frugal conduct. No additional regulations can ever lead to less resource waste, not even if punishments are allowed to be more severe than those that losses already provide. In the long run, all limitations handicap the market's resource optimization mechanism. Entrepreneurs who waste resources and fail to meet the needs of their consumers run out of resources, forcing them to earn a living as wage earners instead, at least until they've accumulated enough capital to give entrepreneurship another try.

"It put me upon reflecting how little repining there would be among mankind at any condition of life, if people would rather compare their condition with those that were worse, in order to be thankful, than be always comparing them with those which are better, to assist their murmurings and complaining."

– Daniel Defoe, *The Life and Adventures of Robinson Crusoe*

10

PROGRESS

Economic progress comes through capital accumulation. The catallactic definition of a progressive economy is "an economy in which the total amount of capital goods increases." Simultaneously, individual goods become cheaper, and new goods arrive on the market to satisfy novel consumer needs. Another way to express this is to say that living standards increase in an economy that progresses. Thanks to the efficiency of the free market process, most of the world's population now own mobile phones — devices that James Bond could only dream of a mere couple of decades ago. No matter how well-educated people are or how advanced their technical skills may be, the economy can only progress if capital goods are available. Savings are crucial to prosperity. We can only increase our living standards by consuming less in the present. And we consume less in the present when we believe that by increasing our savings, we can enjoy more consumption in the future. Entrepreneurs who satisfy customer needs reap the benefits of being profitable without spending their savings. Through market competition, their ability to do so continuously decreases over time. Therefore, to continue enjoying a high standard of living, the entrepreneur *must* innovate and increase production to satisfy more wants and needs. Market competition functions as an imaginary blowtorch aimed at their behinds. Evolve or go out of business. If you manage to evolve, you might avoid being usurped from your entrepreneurial throne by new market actors.

Entrepreneurs acquire additional capital goods in two ways. They can either use their profit to expand whatever technologies they're currently using or invest their profits in developing new ones. Brick producers can acquire more capital by building more brick factories to keep pace with consumer demands. But producers can also choose to invest in automated production, which reduces the cost of human labor and allows them to sell bricks at a lower price. These methods are not mutually exclusive, and both reduce the price of bricks, enabling more people to buy more bricks. Almost every factory requires bricks, so the brick price reduction benefits the production of all other goods *directly* as well as *indirectly*. In the pursuit of profit, the entrepreneur decreases everyone's living costs as a byproduct. In doing so, entrepreneurs free up more time and resources so that others can pursue entrepreneurial careers themselves. Individual capital accumulation is thus paramount for a society to become prosperous.

Critics of capitalism misunderstand the market process because they fail to consider the benefits of profit-seeking entrepreneurial behavior. Most of the misconceptions stem from the fact that most people think that what they're currently living in *is* capitalism, which is not the case in any country. Trigger-happy money-printing institutions are everywhere, and government overreach in markets is the norm, not the exception. The common notion that the capitalist entrepreneur unjustly benefits from the prosperity capital accumulation brings stems from a misunderstanding of how the market process works. We can easily see that entrepreneurs reap only a fraction of what they sow. Profits result from successful risk-taking when trying to satisfy other people's desires. Entrepreneurs will only enjoy profits when they have successfully adjusted their production processes according to the wishes of their consumers. Still, a competitor's increased capital accumulation constantly threatens the entrepreneur's accumulation of profits. Because supply and demand determine prices, every new type of brick introduced on the market lowers the marginal productivity of the factories that produced the original brick. An increased supply of bricks on the market decreases the total value of bricks made in the factories owned by the original producer.

Setting all this aside, let's now focus on the non-entrepreneurial segment of the population. The most magical aspect of the free market process is that, in relative terms, these people are the ones whose living standard increases the most from market competition and decreasing production costs. The marginal productivity of their wage rates and labor goes up regardless of the success of the individual entrepreneur. The purchasing power of a fixed wage always increases over time as long as it's adjusted correctly for monetary inflation. Short term, automation may cause job loss, but because wealth in society has increased, entrepreneurs can afford to employ workers for other tasks and even pay them more. In the imaginary construction of the absolutely free market, capital accumulation and labor division always and necessarily work in everyone's favor. Only when we introduce involuntary, non-consensual action, this ceases to be the case. Non-consensual action includes (but is not limited to) robbery, theft, taxes, market intervention, and money supply manipulation. The market consistently distributes additional wealth created by successful businesses so that the non-entrepreneurial groups benefit without risk of loss. Even laborers employed by competing companies benefit from the success of their competitors since economic competition drives down the prices of all goods. The only population segment with anything to lose from economic progress is unsuccessful entrepreneurs who mismanage their capital and waste resources. Where there is economic progress and the total amount of capital in society increases, the actual wage rates of all workers increase alongside their purchasing power because of the falling prices.

Technological advancements are intrinsic to societal development, but only insofar as society has enough capital to use them. Not having the right tool or technology limits the production of a good. But not having enough capital goods halts the output of that good altogether. Without acquiring the knowledge of how to produce a fishing net, Robinson Crusoe is relegated to catching fish with his bare hands. But even if he figures out how to make a net, he will never be able to produce it unless he's in possession of the necessary raw materials. Only through capital accumulation can Robinson even try to create something new, and only through trial and error can he ascertain whether the fishing net functions as intended. Thus, in the development of a society, the imperative for capital accumulation supersedes technological advancements. The internet can provide you with information about how to acquire almost every skill known to man. But to use those skills, you first need time and capital, which are two sides of the same coin. To build a rocket, you need the parts, and without the necessary materials, a master's degree in rocket science won't even get you to the treetops. Only by accumulating capital can the sky truly be the limit.

Can your earnings buy you more today than they did yesterday? If so, you're making economic progress. Are all prices falling? If true, then society is making economic progress. However, if prices are not decreasing, something is hindering society's economic progress. The intricacies of this hindrance are another matter. But here's a glimpse: Throughout history, those with the power to mint the coin of a country have never resisted the temptation to increase the money supply. Hence, a decrease in the purchasing power of your currency makes the money printer a prime suspect. Systems that interfere with people's ability to save slow economic progress and halt any potential increase in living standards. Envy is the arch-nemesis of progress because it drives people to act against their long-term self-interest by trying to extract value from their fellow human beings using violent, coercive means, such as money printing. The solution is *sound money*, which is costly to produce and, therefore, hard to counterfeit. Sound money is the antidote to the debilitating impact of an increasing money supply as it allows people to protect their capital without having to invest it in risky assets.

Capital accumulation drives progress. Comprehending this reveals the irony inherent in so-called "progressive" politics. The more "progressive" the political movement, the higher the tendency of its proponents to want to hinder actual progress and societal advancement through interference in the market process. It may be true that a "transition to a greener economy" can only be made possible by technological innovation, but innovation plays second fiddle to capital accumulation. Hindering the market process slows the pace of innovation. All tools and technologies have one purpose — to increase efficiency and thereby save time. If those in charge allow the free market to work its magic, everyone benefits from the time-saving. The notion that humans would (or should) voluntarily choose to use *less* energy as we move into the future is naïve and outright dangerous. Our task is to learn to use our available resources more efficiently. The only way to do that is through capital accumulation followed by catallactic competition, which lowers all costs for everyone.

Renewable energy sources are, by definition, more cost-effective than non-renewable ones. But if they need political subsidies and other crutches to appear on the market, they're not renewable. They can't be. If the cost of constructing a solar panel or a wind turbine is higher than the savings one realizes from its final total output, it's not working as advertised. In other words, it wastes more energy than it produces. It really is that simple! We can never calculate actual costs in a market with targeted subsidies, excise duties, and taxes on specific products. Market interventions skew people's notions of actual costs and distort all price signals. In the long run, this is a dangerous game to play because it alters human behavior at its most fundamental level. Politicians reward unproductive, inefficient behavior and punish constructive action by tampering with our incentives to choose one product over another. It is hard to overstate how harmful the effects of market interventionism are since the consequences of unintended side effects are impossible to measure. Because a policy can never be proven successful through empirical evidence, we can only comprehend market phenomena by deductive reasoning.

Further, it is tough to de-program an already brainwashed population. The concentration camps of Nazi Germany and the Gulags of the Soviet Union are stark reminders of what can happen when collectivist fantasies pursue a "greater good for society" directive. The most atrocious crimes ever committed by humans were carried out by people believing their actions effectuated "a greater good," guided by the political narrative du jour. The tragic irony is that everyone would have been better off if they had focused on their own well-being instead of that of the collective.

"This grieved me heartily, and now I saw, though too late, the folly of beginning a work before we count the cost, and before we judge rightly of our own strength to go through with it."

– Daniel Defoe, The Life and Adventures of Robinson Crusoe

11

PRICES

AS WE HAVE SEEN, economic progress results from consensual human interactions in the free market. Those who can see what others don't, the entrepreneurs, initiate the mechanisms that set progress in motion. True, entrepreneurs can make massive profits from improving their production processes, but the poor are the greatest beneficiaries of the increase in capital goods via diminishing prices. We reach these conclusions using deductive reasoning exclusively, starting from a set of irrefutable truths about human action. To understand how prices arise in the market, we must first consider the factors involved in price determination. What forces affect how people evaluate their options and choose whether to purchase something or not? The market is a process that is a product of how people assess their situations and consciously act according to how they value one option over all others in any given case. In analyzing human action, we often use metaphors, which should never be taken literally. Praxeological metaphors are merely illustrations of specific phenomena that result from human conduct.

As discussed earlier, a price is a ratio between two goods. We express the price of a good in terms of the quantity of the good we're exchanging. A price is thus the outcome of two market actors exchanging information about how they value what they get in terms of what they give up. In barter trade, this ratio is all there is to it. In the market, which is a process that arises from the division of labor, more factors are at play. Market participants trade indirectly using a common medium of exchange called money. Money is on one side of all market transactions, allowing market participants to perform economic calculations. A producer of a specific good must find a suitable price for that good to make a profit. The window between the highest and the lowest price he can charge his customers is very narrow. If producers set the price too high, fewer customers will buy the product forcing the producer to keep the excess supply, and storing large amounts of a good is usually a costly affair. If the price is too low, the producer will be unable to keep pace with consumer demands, thereby missing out on potential profits. The producer eventually reaches a point where producing another unit of the good isn't profitable anymore. The more competing producers we add to the mix, the narrower the price window. Thus, the final market price of the good is affected by supply and demand.

Prices indicate where to get the best deals on homogenous goods. Entrepreneurs compete to satisfy their customers' desires by setting the most optimal prices for their goods. The entrepreneur profits when the prices are set low enough to meet demand but high enough to cover the producer's expenses. Price tags set outside this narrow window will result in losses. When selling a good or service is highly profitable, competing actors enter the market and increase supply, ultimately lowering that good's price. When competition is no longer profitable, the price of the good reaches an equilibrium point. Catallactic competition always drives prices toward this theoretical point where no more profit is possible. In reality, though, the equilibrium point does not exist. The market is an ever-changing environment, and any theoretical "all else being equal" -scenario never happens. Like praxeological metaphors, these scenarios are helpful tools for understanding specific market phenomena but are purely imaginary constructs. Through this example, we have explored the mechanisms that dictate the prices of consumer goods. But what about the prices of higher-order goods and factors of production?

Prices emerge because people value things differently. In the case of consumer goods, acting individuals choose to buy because they expect the good or service provided to bring about a more satisfactory state. You buy food with the expectation that eating it will relieve your hunger. Producers analyze the market to determine what they anticipate buyers will pay for the end product. This price must be high enough to cover the total cost of the specific factors of production that went into producing the good but low enough to entice buyers to act. Weighing costs against expected incomes in this way is called appraisement. How well entrepreneurs appraise their future expenses, profits, and losses, affects market prices.

In contrast, the prices of production goods arise from the appraisement of expected utility for the entrepreneur, not from the direct valuation of expected utility, as in the case of consumer goods. All prices stem from consumer valuations, but the value of a thing is not the sum of the value of its parts. A value judgment precedes every human action. Value judgments are, therefore, impossible to sum up mathematically.

The market is a dynamic process, as human activity has no constants. Whatever customers were willing to pay for a product in the past cannot tell us anything specific about what they will pay later. Entrepreneurs can appraise their production processes, but science can't tell us anything specific about future human choices. "Economists" — those who have been "educated" by government-subsidized schools and universities — often claim that human action can be mathematically derived and treat historical prices like empirical evidence for their theories. Unsurprisingly, these so-called economists and their skewed worldviews are very popular among the segments of society that believe they can profit from regulation justified by this supposed evidence. It is easy to see why these flawed theories became so popular if we look at human history since the Age of Enlightenment.

The Enlightenment gave us the scientific method, from which all a-posteriori knowledge stems. Evidence-based, peer-reviewed research led to massive civilizational advancements because it exponentially increased humanity's understanding of our universe and the planet on which we live. The burgeoning scientific community naturally believed they could apply the same methods to studying economics. It wasn't until Ludwig von Mises realized that all economic science is firmly rooted in the subjective valuations governing individual action that praxeology was born. He realized that the only way to conclude anything about human action was to use reason and logical deduction starting from a set of undeniable axioms. Because of the success of the a-posteriori sciences, many scientists question the validity of a-priori knowledge to this day. But the very act of questioning proves the validity of the praxeological axioms. To put something into question in the first place, one must act deliberately out of one's own free will. You cannot question anything without simultaneously proving that human action is purposeful behavior and that you are in possession of your body's faculties.

Throughout the ages, it has been difficult for humans to adopt a bird's eye view of the age in which they live. Humans always think their worldview is "modern" and, for the most part, correct. Science itself can only progress when we dare to question its foundations. The statement, "An increase in the supply of good X will lead to a reduction of its market price if all other factors remain unchanged," does not require empirical evidence. We can conclude that the statement is true using deductive reasoning alone, and empirical evidence can neither further prove nor disprove the claim. To understand human action, we must rid ourselves of all preconceived notions about how to prove scientific claims true or false. As long as the propaganda machines are as powerful as they are today, with government-subsidized media outlets and at least twelve years of mandatory brainwashing in almost every country, changing people's minds is hard. But logical arguments are our only weapon if the pen is indeed mightier than the sword. This author firmly believes that our species' yearning for the truth will eventually triumph and prevent us from destroying ourselves by denying it.

Mainstream economists fear the rise of monopolies on the free market. They claim that an unregulated free market leads to the formation of monopolies, which they define as "businesses that dominate and control the supply of a particular good or service in an industry." But what constitutes a particular good? Because of the subjective nature of value judgments, it is impossible to quantify what the concept of "a particular good" means to another person. As discussed earlier, a person may be willing to pay more for a car if he buys it from a friend. Likewise, a person may prefer one brand over another, even if the product comes from the same factory. Observing that two goods are physically identical can not tell the observer anything about how a particular customer will value them. A worn-out teddy bear that an adult loved as a child is probably worth more to that person than a new one of the same kind. In short, human valuations cannot be cardinally ranked or measured. Therefore, it is also impossible to identify which companies have a monopoly on which goods and services since only the individual actor can decide what constitutes a particular good to them. The definition becomes so broad that the word "monopoly" loses all meaning when defined in this way. The Coca-Cola Company may have a monopoly on selling Coca-Cola to a particular bar or restaurant. Still, as long as the consumer can choose to visit another establishment or order a different beverage, this definition of monopoly is practically pointless.

The same logic applies to the false notion of monopoly prices. In the free market, all exchanges are voluntary. A person can always abstain from purchasing a specific good or service. "Monopoly prices" is a popular term among mainstream economists who define it as "when a seller can increase his profit by restricting the supply and raise the price above what it would have been if he had market competitors." But there are always competitors in a free market. If a town has only one egg provider, and that provider sets the price too high, people can choose to consume fewer eggs or even switch to having bacon instead of eggs for breakfast. All market producers compete to exchange their goods and services for one particular good — money.

As a society's capital accumulation increases, the market supplies the end consumer with an increasing number of options. Even if a giant corporation devours all of its competitors, it still can't set monopoly prices. People can start businesses for the sole purpose of being acquired by a larger corporation, and every time this is done, that corporation loses money. The only way for a company to "drive out the competition" would be to set their prices so low that newcomers couldn't compete with them. But this is precisely why competition is so good for the consumer. Amazon and Walmart may have driven out competitors by offering insanely low prices, but the game is on again as soon as they raise them. Ultimately, this benefits consumers. Even if the alleged monopoly drives a smaller company to bankruptcy, that company's stock of capital goods remains intact and up for grabs for a modest price. This stock of cheap production goods allows for more efficient competition as some new market actor will likely purchase and deploy them eventually. "Monopoly prices" is thus a term born out of financial illiteracy — all prices are competitive since they all compete with all other prices.

The apparent absence of monopolies in the imaginary construct of the absolutely free market begs the question — do monopolies even exist? Unfortunately, yes. A business can find itself in a monopoly position whenever it's allowed to dominate an industry through coercive, violent means. Criminal enterprises can achieve monopolies and force their competitors out of business by threatening these competitors' families. But this unfair advantage is not limited to mobs, gangs, and mafias. Monopolies can and do form wherever there is market interventionism — an excise duty on a specific good will drive out competition, as will a government subsidy on another. Artificially low interest rates, resulting from an artificial increase in a country's money supply, disproportionately favor big companies and drive smaller ones out of business. Ever-changing regulations favor those that can afford to keep up with them and are rarely helpful to smaller companies. In short, any policy that interferes with the market process reduces overall market competition, giving already established actors an unfair advantage. Primarily since all market actors ultimately compete for the same good — money.

"I smil'd to myself at the sight of this money, O drug! said I aloud, what art thou good for? Thou art not worth to me, no not the taking off of the ground, one of those knives is worth all this heap, I have no manner of use for thee, e'en remain where thou art, and go to the bottom as a creature whose life is not worth saving. However, upon second thoughts, I took it away..."

– Daniel Defoe, The Life and Adventures of Robinson Crusoe

12

PURCHASING POWER

Nothing is as crucial to the functionality of a free market as its money. Money constitutes half of all value expressed through exchanging goods and services in an economy. So what is the price of money? As explained earlier, the commodity with the highest saleability in a market quickly becomes that market's preferred medium of exchange, a fancy way of saying that it becomes its money. Market prices denominated in this good allow for economic calculation, which is necessary for society to advance. When and wherever there's a discrepancy between prices, there's an opportunity for entrepreneurs to make profits. We've seen how supply and demand determine the price of goods, but determining the price of money is a bit trickier. Our predicament is that we have no unit of account to measure the price of money because we already express prices in, you guessed it, money. And because we cannot use monetary terms to explain it, we must find another way to express money's purchasing power.

People sell and buy money for the value they believe that money can bring them in the form of goods and services at a later time. Acting individuals always make choices on the margin, hence the law of diminishing marginal utility. In other words, all actions are preceded by a value judgment in which actors choose between their most valued end and their next strongest desire. The utility of money is no different from any other good or service in this regard. A person determines a sum of money's utility by the marginal utility of adding a unit of the particular good or service he believes this sum of money will buy him to his already existing stock. The same forces that determine the prices of every good on the market, supply and demand, also determine the purchasing power of money. The cost of money in an exchange is the highest utility a person could have derived from the amount of cash they gave up. If a person chooses to work for an hour to afford a rib-eye steak, they must value the meal more than one hour of forgone leisure.

Recall that the law of diminishing marginal returns tells us that each successive unit of a homogenous good satisfies a less urgent desire a person has. Therefore, the value a person attaches to an additional unit diminishes for each unit added. However, what constitutes a homogenous good is entirely up to the individual. To the individual, each extra coin is not homogenous in terms of what serviceability it brings to them. To a person who wishes to buy nothing but hot dogs with his money, a "unit of money" is the same as whatever the price of a hot dog is. That person has not added a unit of the homogenous good "money for hot dogs" until he has acquired enough cash to buy one more hot dog. The money Robinson Crusoe found on the derelict ship that once brought him to the island was useless to him because it couldn't buy him anything. Money is, first and foremost, a tool for communication — a language. Like all other languages, money requires more than one human being to be useful.

People choose to save, spend, or invest money based on their time preference and what they predict that money's purchasing power will be in the future. If they expect their money's purchasing power to go up, the incentive to save it for a later date becomes stronger. If, on the other hand, they expect its purchasing power to diminish, their motivation to spend it increases. Investing alters this analysis slightly, as a person's expectation of money's future purchasing power also influences what type of investments that person chooses to make. Regardless of individual predictions of money's future value, money kept, whether saved or invested, provides the keeper with a specific service — it lowers uncertainty. By keeping money, one forgoes one's ability to satisfy other desires for the satisfaction of one's desire for safety. There is no way of distinguishing money hoarded from money intended to fulfill more immediate ends.

For this reason, money is never "in circulation" since it is always in the hands of a specific owner. Remember the praxeological definition of "the present" — the temporal period in which an actor evaluates, chooses, and acts. An exchange is an action; all actions happen at a particular moment. The money is thus always owned by someone and never "circulates." Cash can never flow in the same sense that a river flows. It can only switch owners at exact points. Money is never idle but is always of some service to its owner. The only way for a person to properly evaluate their money's future purchasing power is by studying historical prices. To do so, one must consider how much various goods and services cost today compared to what they cost in the past. Only then can a person get a clue as to whether prices are inflating or deflating.

Governmental institutions often provide their subjects with a "Consumer Price Index," which supposedly measures inflation. They base this number on a basket of goods composed of a fixed set of groceries and how the prices of these goods change over time. But measuring inflation this way is an attempt to hide the truth about inflation — the increase in prices is always proportional to the expansion of the money supply eventually. The creation of new money always leads to a decrease in the purchasing power of that money compared to what it could have been. As discussed before, if prices increase over time, people have a stronger incentive to spend than save money. Those who wish to retain their capital tend to buy assets they believe will maintain their value better than money. When measuring inflation, the money issuers purposefully exclude high-value assets from the CPI basket of goods. Otherwise, the prices of stocks, bonds, fine art, and real estate would reveal an inconvenient truth — that inflation is always way higher than the general public believes.

Inflation's impact on society is sinister and insidious. An increase in the money supply always favors those who hold assets and those closest to the monetary spigot. Even worse, price increases lag actual inflation and are felt by those they affect the most after the damage is already done.

Monetary inflation effectively funnels wealth from the poor to the rich. However, even the super-rich would have been better off if those in charge of the money printers could resist the urge to use them. The free market benefits all segments of society in the long run, and the freer it is, the better it functions.

If, at each moment, the only way to predict money's future purchasing power is by studying historical prices, what was money's initial worth? By looking in the rearview mirror, we eventually arrive at a time when a common medium of exchange first emerged in the barter economy. What later evolved into today's money must have offered some additional value to people beyond its usefulness as money at some point. The purchasing power of the good that evolved into money must have been determined solely by consumer and commercial demand. At the exact moment someone used that specific good as money for the first time, the demand for it increased. It now served two distinct purposes for the owner — providing utility value on the one hand and functioning as a medium of exchange on the other. The need for the latter use case tends to overshadow the former over time.

These co-demands set the purchasing power of all monetary goods. Gold, for instance, is used by jewelers and has some industrial use, but most people value it because of its historic role as a store of value. At one point, even our bank accounts and the numbers representing money on a screen were redeemable for gold. Fiat currencies came into existence when people started trading receipts for gold instead of carrying around heavy metal coins that were difficult to transport. The lightweight and compact banknote proved the perfect solution to gold's transportability problem. Unfortunately, the issuers of these receipts quickly realized they could issue more gold tickets (banknotes) than they had backing for in their vaults. Indeed, over-issuance is a problem that persists and has worsened over time. Today, banks that cannot repay their debts need not file for bankruptcy if they are politically connected enough to get bailed out.

Money's temporal connection to historical prices is vital for the market process. Without it, personal economic calculations would be impossible. The *Money Regression Theorem*, described in the previous section, is a praxeological insight often overlooked in discussions about money. It explains why money is not just an imaginary construct by some bureaucratic wizardry but has a real connection to a point when someone's desire to trade means for a specific end spawned it into existence in the free market. Money is a product of voluntary exchange, not a political invention or a social contract; a money printer, on the other hand, is. Only by understanding the origins of money can we comprehend the dangers of tampering with its supply.

Any commodity with a limited enough supply could be used as money, presuming it ticked off all the other boxes necessary for a suitable medium of exchange. Anything durable, portable, divisible, uniform, and acceptable will do. Suppose the Mona Lisa had been infinitely divisible. In that case, its parts could have served as money, but only if there was an easy way to verify that they were actually from the Mona Lisa and not counterfeited. Speaking of the Mona Lisa, there's an anecdote about some of the most famous painters of the twentieth century that perfectly illustrates how an increase in the supply of a monetary good affects its perceived value. These painters realized they could use their celebrity status to enrich themselves in a peculiar way. They figured out that their signatures were valuable and that they could pay their restaurant bills by simply signing them. Salvador Dali allegedly even signed the wreck of a car that he had crashed into and thus magically transformed it into a valuable piece of art. But after a while, these tactics stopped working. The more signed bills, posters, and car wrecks there were, the less valuable an additional signature became, perfectly demonstrating the law of diminishing returns. By adding quantity, they reduced quality.

We can observe the same phenomenon in all fiat currencies. When their supply is increased, their value decreases. True, the increase may temporarily enrich the issuer and the first receivers of the new supply. Still, the people on the bottom always pay the people on top of the pyramid in schemes like these. Fiat currency is the biggest pyramid scheme ever known to man. Inflation acts as a hidden tax that disproportionately punishes the poorest segments of society. The only way to stop it is to refuse to use government-issued currencies.

"Man is a short-sighted creature, sees but a very little way before him, and as his passions are none of his best friends, so his particular affections are generally his worst counselors."

– Daniel Defoe, *The Life and Adventures of Robinson Crusoe*

13

TIME PREFERENCE

As we have learned, the praxeological notion of "the present" differs from other scientific disciplines' definitions. In praxeology, the present encompasses the entirety of the action — the time absorbed by choice of action, the act itself, and its completion. Completion can bring utility or disutility to the actor, but this is irrelevant to the praxeological definition of what "the present" means to the individual actor. In the empirical sciences, the present refers to a specific point in time — in physics, it can even represent a particular point in space-time. The price of action, praxeologically speaking, is always described in terms of opportunity costs. We cannot measure the cost of an action by measuring lost time alone. What options that are available to a person change from moment to moment, and thus, so do the opportunity costs for choosing to do one thing over another. This causal, temporal relationship is what separates praxeological time from measurable time. The extended presence of action consists of two sub-steps — working time and waiting time. Working time is when the acting individual uses physical labor to achieve his goal. Waiting time is the period between the point where the physical struggle stops and the moment the actor reaches his desired end. The total sum of the two steps is called *the period of production*.

It is easy to see that the act of growing a crop consists of planting the seed (working time) and letting it grow and bear fruit (waiting time). But even a much more instant act, such as drinking a beverage, has a working time and a waiting time. The drinker lifts the glass, pours the drink into his mouth, and swallows it (working time). Only then does he evaluate whether the desired end (presumably thirst-quenching) was reached. There's always a waiting time in the extended present of human action. The period of production must always be accounted for because action implies choosing one thing to do over another. Even if a person had enough money to buy all the theme parks in the world and enough leisure to spend the rest of their life at these places, they would still have to choose one action at a time. One cannot simultaneously visit Disneyland and Disney World.

Acting individuals consider whatever means they have in the present and act according to what they think those means will yield them in the future. Past means cannot be affected by present means. Their experiences can teach them how to make better choices, but they cannot change the past. All actions aim toward future goals. In acting, we sometimes only consider the impending moment and sometimes a more distant point in the future. The time horizon for which people think about the future implications of their decisions is called *the period of provision*. *The duration of serviceability* is the period in which the desired end will continue to satisfy the consumer. Together, these time factors play a role in action evaluations and decisions. Let's assemble them for closer inspection:

1. The period of production (labor time and waiting time)
2. The period of provision (the time all intermediate actions take)
3. The duration of serviceability (how long the final product is useful)

To illustrate how an actor evaluates time factors, we will consider the case of a forty-six-year-old man who decides to write a book about praxeology. Before he starts writing, he will consider how long it will take him to write the book and weigh it against all the other things he could have done instead. He will also factor in how long that book will be of service to him, including (but not limited to) whatever yield it will bring him in terms of money. After all, writing a book can bring much more satisfaction than mere financial gains. Lastly, he will consider how writing this book will play into his entire array of decision-making. Will sacrificing the time he could have spent with his family free up more time for him to spend with them at a later date? Will the process of writing this book make writing books easier for him in the future? Will the readers enjoy the book and give it positive reviews, enabling him to sell more of his previous books too? Well? Will the recognition he can gain from the book increase his options in the future? All of these are time factors that he has to take into more or less consideration before deciding to sit down and start writing.

All actors aim for the satisfaction of a specific act to come sooner rather than later. To claim otherwise would be absurd. The act of saving is not postponing everything indefinitely. People do it because it reduces uncertainty in the present, not because they never wish to consume at all. How willing a person is to delay the gratification gained from action is called *time preference*. A person with a high time preference prioritizes short-time goals, whereas a person with a low time preference is more patient. A person's time preference can never be zero, as that would imply a willingness to postpone everything forever. Everyone has a time preference greater than zero, and we call this *the universal fact of time preference*. People always prefer an additional unit of a homogenous good sooner rather than later. But what counts as homogeneity is entirely up to the individual actor. An actor may decide not to buy a green apple immediately but instead wait for the store to stock up on red apples. In this case, the actor does not consider *apples* per se homogenous but instead sees homogeneity only in red apples. Homogeneity in monetary goods is often referred to as fungibility (or uniformity) — one of the six properties of money. Money must be fungible so that a bank note is worth the same amount of coins as the figure printed on it claims. However, whether money is fungible or not is not binary.

On November 8, 2016, the government of India announced the demonetization of all 500-Rupee and 1000-Rupee banknotes in use at the time. It also issued new banknotes that people could exchange for the demonetized ones. The government claimed its main objective was to curb the usage of black money, which included unreported and thus untaxed income. The people of India kept using the old banknotes, but their value dropped over time.

An example of the opposite effect can be found in *Monopoly* money. A 1935 Trade Mark Edition Monopoly board game box set is worth somewhere between $400 and $1000 today. The box contains around twenty thousand units of toy money, making each monopoly dollar worth between two and five cents. Considering that the game's original 1935 price was about two dollars, we can conclude that those monopoly dollars have stored value orders of magnitude better than "real" dollars. Not to mention the New York museum that once paid $146,500 for one of the original five thousand copies of the original, handmade version of the game.

Alright, back to time preference. When people grow up and have kids, their perspective of time often changes. They realize that they'll need to get their lives together if they're going to be able to support their families. Children usually have a higher time preference than their parents. They are yet to develop the necessary skills to predict their actions' outcomes. In a sense, lowering one's time preference is what growing up is. It's about taking responsibility for your actions. People's time preference also often rises again towards the end of their lives as they realize how little time they have left, especially if they don't have any children. The point is that time preference is personal and dynamic, like everything else in human action.

The yield one acquires by engaging in a production process differs from process to process, but the more time one devotes to producing a good, the higher the potential returns. Before entering a long production period, one must accumulate enough capital to satisfy all intermediate, more urgent needs. Say that Robinson Crusoe wishes to build a canoe to catch fish in the ocean and not only in the pond. To free up the time needed to create a canoe, he must first stockpile food to eat during the construction process. To save enough fish, he first needs to make a net, which, as explained earlier, he can only do by first catching enough fish with his hands to commence that production process. Shorter production processes precede lengthier ones in this way. Because of this, people must lower their time preferences to start a more prolonged process. In other words, they have to delay their consumption of present goods. By reducing your time preference, you speed up your process of capital accumulation. Increased capital accumulation and lengthier, higher-yielding production processes raise the marginal utility of labor. Put another way: the more sophisticated the production process is, the more efficient the man-hour becomes. Higher wages and more employment soon follow—the productivity of land, labor, and capital increase as society lowers its time preference. The more capital people have, the closer in time they are to achieving their goals. In this sense, capital is time stored up. The more capital you have, the less consumption you'll have to give up to reach your goals.

Another thing to consider when analyzing time preference and capital accumulation is the convertibility of capital goods. If a producer realizes that his productive efforts will not bear the fruit he predicted, he might choose to repurpose the capital goods to produce something else. The more primitive the capital good is, the easier this is to do. The more specific purpose the capital good has, the more expensive it becomes to convert it into something that can be useful in another production process. Robinson Crusoe can easily repurpose the rope intended for the fishing net. It is harder for him to find a substitute use case for the canoe.

Similarly, a purpose-built circuit for a specific industrial robot may be entirely non-convertible. Capital goods are innately conservative in this way. They best fit the purpose for which someone initially built them. Despite this potential drawback, lengthier production processes are still more productive; the more advanced the machinery used, the higher the output of consumer goods. The convertibility of a capital good determines when producers will replace it without regard for the availability of new fancy technologies. People will only replace something old with something new after accumulating enough capital to try out the latest technology. Capital accumulation is paramount for producers and consumers to advance. People don't automatically replace their old car just because a more advanced one is available, and car manufacturers don't automatically erect robotic giga-factories.

Setting capital convertibility aside, let us focus on what outside forces might affect a person's time preference instead. A person with no belongings must adopt a high time preference to survive. A person with all his belongings stolen finds himself in this situation. When you have nothing, you must prioritize your most basic needs. Finding food and shelter will overrule any other desires on your value scale.

In contrast, when you have a lot of capital, you can afford to adopt a low time preference and focus on long-term goals. But even if you have merely a tiny part of your belongings taken away, theft *always* affects your time preference. There's a clear connection between what you have and how ambitious your dreams can be. Who the robber is doesn't matter — when someone deprives you of your belongings, you must regress into a comparatively more primitive mode of living. If someone regularly forces you to give up parts of what you own, like when you pay taxes, you might never advance because you must constantly forgo your long-term plans. The damage this does to society is immeasurable, even in countries with "modest" taxes. Plus, we never get to see what could have been.

An apple farmer who owns one single apple tree might profit so much from selling apples that he can afford an additional tree the following year. Now he can satisfy the desires of twice as many consumers. If the process is allowed to continue, the apple farmer can double the size of his business every year, engage in catallactic competition, increase productivity, reduce prices, and make life better for everyone at an exponential pace. But if he has to give up half his profit in taxes, he will never even get to the second tree! And no one will ever know what could have been. The alternative timeline never reveals itself. There is no empirical evidence to support praxeological theories. Only through understanding human action from a-priori axioms can we comprehend time preference and how detrimental to society scheduled theft can be.

"I had more care upon my head now than I had in my state of life in the island where I wanted nothing but what I had, and had nothing but what I wanted; whereas I had now a great charge upon me, and my business was how to secure it. I had not a cave now to hide my money in, or a place where it might lie without lock or key, till it grew mouldy and tarnished before anybody would meddle with it; on the contrary, I knew not where to put it, or whom to trust with it."

– Daniel Defoe, *The Life and Adventures of Robinson Crusoe*

14

LOANS AND INTEREST

As we've learned, acting individuals always prefer satisfying the same end sooner rather than later, and we call this the *universal law of time preference*. One can only create or save capital by lowering one's time preference and rising above one's instinctual urges. Under this scenario, the market functions correctly, and society advances. Capital goods are necessary for the production of consumer goods. The more productive the capital good, the closer in time the end product. Because capital goods result from man mixing his labor with the natural resources around him to create tools, we can view them as stored-up time. Every device or technology made by a human being was made for one specific purpose — to save time. In praxeology, time and capital are interchangeable terms. Time is money, literally. More capital enables an entrepreneur to be closer in time to his desired ends. For an entrepreneurial venture to be profitable, the cost of the production cannot exceed the product's final price. Further, the capital goods involved in the production process must be sufficiently productive for this to be the case. In a mature market economy, almost all production requires indirect exchange, making money itself a capital good. Moreover, money is the most convertible capital good since you can exchange it for every other good on the market. In this sense, money is time stored.

Workers typically earn salaries that are disproportionate to the earnings of their employer. Workers accept a lower, fixed salary contract in exchange for the certainty steady employment brings. In this instance, the entrepreneur takes on more risk than the worker and can sometimes reap higher rewards. Entrepreneurs must also be capitalists since they must generate savings to facilitate production. In response to profitability threats from market dynamism and catallactic competition, they must also continually analyze market data and adapt their processes accordingly. Nimble adjustments are necessary as a dynamic market produces a degree of unpredictability. At the same time, catallactic competition causes market prices to trend toward an equilibrium, which constitutes the hypothetical end price for a specific good or service. No risk, no reward.

In the imaginary scenario of a world in which an entrepreneurial venture could bring no more profits or losses, in other words, a world without risk, the business owner would no longer be an entrepreneur. But he would still be a capitalist. All production processes require capital goods, also called factors of production. Even in a world without uncertainty, saving capital is the only way to provide time, labor, and land to produce a consumer good. The capitalist is the workers' time supplier. An investment is effectively a trade in which the capitalist sells a present good, a sum of money, for an anticipated future good that he believes he can sell for more money later. By this point, it should be clear that all goods have a current price lower than the future price of that same good. Obviously, this same logic applies to money too, which is why the concept of *interest* exists.

A time trade tells us a couple of things about the two interacting parties. If a capitalist loans one hundred units of money to be paid back within a year plus an extra five units of that same money, we call the additional five percent the *annual interest rate*. The loan giver is expressing that he is willing to trade away the certainty of having access to those one hundred units of money during the term of the loan for the profit of five units of money he expects the loan taker to give him in the future. He also expresses that his time preference is lower than that of the loan taker, who, through his action, tells us that he values money in the present more than money in the future. Without time preference trades like this one, all workers employed by a producer would have to wait until the product was finished and sold on the market before they could get their wages. We can define a wage as a discounted good in the form of money that employees accept as a substitute for whatever yield their labor could have brought them in the future. The capitalists' primary function is to supply time. Their capital stock is like a sorcerer's mana pool in a computer game — a source of magic that they can use to buff their fellow gamers' stats to make progress in the game.

Trying to eliminate the time element from economic theory is a fool's errand. Production fails without capital goods, and capital goods represent time economically. Any economic theory that tries to remove capitalism from the market process misses the point about capital. When money functions correctly, time truly is money. There is no way around this. The premium of the return of a capital good is the value of time determined by the price spread through each production process. We call this *the Rate of Interest*. The time market consists of more than the market for money loans. It necessarily includes all capital goods since all capital goods are time investments. If we imagine a world without risk, we can isolate the capitalists' exact role in a production structure.

A world without risk would be a world without money, though. In reality, all capitalists producing any good or service are simultaneously entrepreneurs since all production and profit-seeking require risk-taking. Entrepreneurs must consider both time and interest rates. Interest rates are affected by opportunity costs, risks, and the uncertainty of the entrepreneurs who want to take on risk by lending money. Just as prices trend toward equilibria, the market typically converges on a specific interest rate. If one bank's interest rate is much lower than another's, a clever entrepreneur will borrow from the former bank and lend to the latter. Supply and demand underpin interest rates too, and arbitrage opportunities disappear over time because people compete to exploit them.

There is no such thing as a negative time preference. People always prefer stuff sooner rather than later. The market interest rate results from the competing time preferences of people buying and selling time on the market and can never be negative. It is the ratio between the average market desirability of goods in the present and goods in the future. Therefore, the market's pure interest rate is more than just the price of borrowing money. It derives from the genuine scarcity of actual goods, not just the amount of money available on the market. Because praxeology includes time as a factor of production, it exposes why inflating the money supply cannot bring down actual interest rates without requiring other people to pay for cheap loans through rising consumer prices of goods and services. Artificially lowered interest rates do not, and cannot, add anything to the overall economy. All they can do is funnel resources from the have-nots to the haves and reduce the market process's functionality. The illusion of progress is not progress.

"My father, a wise and grave man, gave me serious and excellent counsel against what he foresaw was my design."

– Daniel Defoe, *The Life and Adventures of Robinson Crusoe*

15

CAPITAL THEORY

INTEREST is a phenomenon that arises from the fact that humans act and therefore prefer the same satisfaction sooner rather than later. It is not merely the price of a loan but an expression of an undeniable truth about human existence — that we all have a time preference. We've also learned that a person's time preference cannot be zero, as that would imply complete inaction and death. Man must act, period. From these undeniable starting points, we've reasoned ourselves to further insights and concluded that capital accumulation is a necessary precursor to economic growth. Using these insights, we can now form a coherent theory about how the mechanics of the free market lead to prosperity. Through deductive reasoning and the praxeological way of thinking, we can fully explore the importance of time preference and its connection to civilizational advancement.

Let's break down, step-by-step, what happens to society when people voluntarily lower their time preferences. To do that, we'll use an imaginary construct once again. This time, let's imagine an economy without gains or losses. What will happen to that economy when people start saving voluntarily? The answer is threefold.

1. The lowering of time preference.
2. A decrease in interest rates.
3. A change in the relationship between capital and labor.

First, let's lay out what a general lowering of time preferences means. Another way of putting it is a general increase in savings and investment and a reduction of immediate consumption. In our imaginary construct of the profit- and loss-free economy, a general lowering of people's time preferences begins when that society's net savings surpass its net consumption. The first effect we observe after people start saving is a general lowering of consumer prices. Remember: praxeology is an a-priori science — we do not need to observe anything to draw conclusions, but for now, let's use the term *observation* anyway. When individuals reduce their present consumption, sellers of consumer goods must lower their prices and reduce their profit margin to avoid going out of business. The closer producers are to the final consumer product, the greater impact this effect will have on them.

Interestingly, producers of capital goods and factors of production will not be immediately affected by the drop in consumer prices; they will absorb this impact later as the effects cascade through the market. By reducing consumption, buyers signal to the market that they prefer quality over quantity. At the same time, decreasing profits incentivize entrepreneurial investment in more profitable stages of production, those found further away from the final product. This relocation of capital adds steps to production and spawns advances in later stages, resulting in better consumer products. Predictably, additional voluntary savings will end up in stages further away from consumption, resulting in lengthier structures of production, which leads to more and better goods on the market. This capital relocation process will continue until the new rate of general time preference in society has spread uniformly across all production sectors. In other words, if all the Robinson Crusoes of the world save enough money to buy fishing nets, the market will provide them with these nets. And if all the Robinson Crusoes increase their savings, the market would ultimately respond by offering them an improvement to their nets, possibly even robotic trawlers.

Decreasing interest rates is the second effect of a general decline in time preference. As we've learned, interest rates are simply the ratio between the prices of present goods against future goods. It should come as no surprise that in a world where people value delayed gratification, market competition for loans increases, and interest rates drop. An entrepreneur evaluates a capital good based on the marginal productivity of that good for producing consumer goods. In other words, the price of a capital good trends toward the present value of its expected future productivity. Analyzing these phenomena together, we can see that lower interest rates lead to an increase in the general productivity of capital goods.

When a society increases its savings, the production process lengthens, and the number of stages in the production process grows. Such changes increase the average duration of serviceability for capital goods. Again — quality over quantity. The lower interest rates increase the prices of capital goods as their marginal productivity increases. Thus, lowered interest rates allow previously unprofitable ventures to become profitable, incentivizing entrepreneurs to start producing more advanced goods.

Let's illustrate by imagining Robinson Crusoe again. This time, Robinson is no longer a marooned loner but a struggling fisherman in a productive economy. If that economy has a low savings rate, interest rates are kept high, and Robinson might be unable to afford a loan for a bigger boat. In this case, the yearly returns of a larger fishing boat are lower than the cost of borrowing money on the market. If there's a high general rate of savings, on the other hand, interest rates are low, and loans are thus cheap to repay. In this scenario, Robinson can expand his business by buying a bigger boat. A bigger boat is an example of a new, more advanced, and thus lengthier, production process. The acquisition of the bigger boat is called a *vertical deepening* of a production structure. If Robinson had instead used the opportunity of the lowered interest rates to expand his fleet with additional smaller boats, he would have *horizontally widened* his production structure.

To sum up, a general increase in savings leads to more competition in the loan market, lowering the going rate of interest. Lower interest rates mean lower prices for consumer goods and increased prices for capital goods in proportion to their distance from consumption. The increased value of the capital goods, in turn, leads to an expansion of the general production structure, either vertically or horizontally. New, lengthier processes become profitable, and existing ones can expand and increase production. What is the net outcome of lowered time preferences? Cheaper, more advanced consumer goods and services. A general lowering of time preference also affects the stock market. When society increases its savings, companies that handle production stages far from consumption go up in value, while companies in the consumer goods sector experience a temporary relative decline.

The third effect of a general drop in time preference concerns the relationship between capital and labor. As consumer prices decrease, every worker's wage now buys them more goods. In other words — their real wages increase. Real wages depend on money's purchasing power, which goes up when society advances. That is, as long as the counterfeiters of the central banks can resist the urge to let their printers run amok. Sadly enough, they almost never can. The flip side of an increase in real wages for workers is the loss of profit for entrepreneurs who produce consumer goods. For them, labor has become relatively more expensive, and to adjust, they often replace workers with machines and automation. If capital becomes cheaper than labor, entrepreneurs tend to invest in more capital-intensive and, therefore, more advanced production stages. Low-time-preference societies thus become more advanced than high-time-preference ones.

To illustrate — long winters force people to think more long-term, which alludes to why countries without them, from a historical perspective, have not progressed technologically as fast as their colder counterparts. Labor and capital goods always compete with one another. Capital goods replace labor when the latter becomes comparatively more expensive. Robinson Crusoe's trawler competes with his catching-fish-by-hand work in the lake, just as e-mail competes with the postman. As savings rise and society advances, the demand for higher-skilled labor rises, and the demand for unskilled labor shrinks.

All of this is not to be confused with artificial market interventionism, which can sometimes superficially produce the same effects. The touch screens in your local McDonald's that have replaced the waiters are mostly there because of counter-productive minimum wage laws — not because of actual technological progress. "Negative interest rates" don't really exist but are paid for by excessive money printing, and future generations will have to foot the bill at some point. Electric car companies are highly valued because they're subsidized and can easily get their hands on these cheap artificial loans — not because they're "the technology of the future."

Praxeological capital theory shows us the logical steps that follow when people generally lower their time preferences and start thinking more long-term. The inevitable outcome of the phenomena explained in this chapter is an increase in consumer goods supplied through lengthier production structures. Things will become cheaper, more advanced, and more abundant, benefiting everyone, especially those with a low income. Today, a one-dollar-a-day worker in a developing country can access a broader array of better tools than any millionaire did a hundred years ago. Most of these tools are on his smartphone. A modern smartphone typically provides its owner a telephone, a GPS, and a flashlight but also access to the entire internet and everything on it.

Books, movies, newspapers, music albums, and tv-shows are all trending toward zero in terms of cost to the consumer. The only price you pay for listening to a song or a book today is the time you must allocate to listening, except for a small streaming service fee and whatever you pay your internet service provider. The smartphone is a truly remarkable example of what a global free market can spawn. Even in the pseudo-free market of the twenty-first century, technological deflation has made many products accessible to almost everyone on the planet. The notion that a market functions best when inflationary currencies encourage people to spend more is false and dangerous. The smartphone emerged from the market despite people using inflationary currencies, not because of them.

Economic progress in a free market leads to a drop in money prices as production and transportation costs decrease over time. As we've learned and can observe in our lives, economic progress happens exponentially. Because of this, prices ought to drop exponentially, too. Some prices have, like the cost of data storage per megabyte, for instance. Few people realize, though, that it's not only the realm of computing that has grown exponentially more cost-efficient — every industry on Earth has. The cost of producing and shipping an avocado to another country is orders of magnitude lower than a decade ago. More progress has happened in the economy during the last ten years than in the previous fifty. The only reason prices remain somewhat "stable," rather than decrease, is the dilution of the global money supply. This monetary dilution must accelerate because of the exponential nature of economic progress. All money printing leads to is a constant funneling of wealth from the already empty pockets of the masses into the already abysmally deep pockets of those closest to the currency spigots.

"I found in this seaman's chest about fifty pieces of eight, in rials, but no gold: I supposed this belonged to a poorer man than the other, which seemed to belong to some officer."

– Daniel Defoe, *The Life and Adventures of Robinson Crusoe*

16

COUNTERFEITING

Now that we've studied how a saleable good becomes money on the free market and how low-time-preference thinking advances society and makes everything cheaper for everyone, we can examine how *money* works today. You may have noticed that some countries experience "negative interest rates" and perhaps wondered how to square negative interest rates with the fact that there's no such thing as negative time preference. You may also have noticed the accelerating inflation rate and mainstream media outlets blaming this phenomenon on everything but money printing. The truth about modern money is a hard pill to swallow because once you understand the magnitude of the problem, things start looking pretty bleak. Yet the truth about money printing is simple — human beings cannot resist the urge to enrich themselves by exploiting others through printing money.

The United Kingdom was the first country to loosen the connection between gold and its national currency. Before the first world war, almost all currencies were redeemable for their worth in gold, which emerged as the most saleable good on the market over five thousand years ago. By 1971, gold convertibility was scrapped entirely when President Richard M. Nixon decided that prolonging the Vietnam War to win another election was so important that the United States should finance it with counterfeit money. Many books describe the dysfunctionality of the fiat monetary paradigm, and we will not deep-dive into the matter here. What we need to know are the basics — state-issued currency is not money; it is debt. Every new Dollar, Euro, and Yuan magically comes into being when a big bank grants an investor a loan, and the investor eventually has to pay the money back with interest. Thus, there is never enough money available on the market.

On top of this, national central banks further manipulate the money supply through bailouts, which prevents certain other banks from going out of business when they should, as well as sometimes conjuring up even more currency through *quantitative easing*. Quantitative easing is when the state gives the central bank a government bond and gets freshly printed greenbacks in return. A government bond is a promise from the government to repay, with interest, the money they just summoned from nowhere. Embedded in the bond is the government's commitment to keep taking your stuff through taxes and steal even more in the future while you and your heirs are forced to cope with rising prices.

Money printing perpetuates the delusional philosophy of *Keynesianism*, the economic theory on which modern governments base their policies. According to Keynesians, the best way to solve a societal problem is to pretend it doesn't exist and print more money to keep government employees working. They claim that whenever a dollar bill changes hands, a dollar's worth of value gets added to the overall economy. They fail to realize that you cannot add value to society by diluting the value of money. If we add a zero to every dollar in existence, the value of a dollar would be a tenth of whatever it was the day before. As we've learned, economies grow because people trade with others and their future selves. They accumulate capital and plan for the future, producing more and cheaper products for everyone. You cannot fake this process by printing more money. What happens instead is the opposite — an ever-changing purchasing power of money makes economic calculations harder and slows down progress.

All government-issued fiat currencies eventually die. They die either through hyperinflation or because the government decides to replace the national one with a more international one (like Euros or Dollars.) During its lifespan, a fiat currency funnels wealth very efficiently from the hands of productive people into the hands of politically well-connected people. The further from the newly minted cash you are, the more you pay for the whole ordeal. The original, or initial, recipients of new money enjoy higher living standards at the expense of later recipients. The concept of relative inflation, or a disproportionate price rise among different economic goods, is known as the *Cantillon Effect*, first described by Irish economist Richard Cantillon about three hundred years ago. It's not exactly breaking news that being poor in a fiat economy is expensive.

Politicians, central bankers, and government-funded, university-educated "economists" continue to proclaim that a certain inflation rate is necessary for the economy to function. Still, those who have studied praxeology know that this is a lie. We see through the lies and conclude that anyone who asserts that monetary inflation is good for the economy is either misinformed, confused, or outright malevolous. Sometimes all three. We've deductively reasoned ourselves to the conclusion that counterfeiting does not lead to prosperity. We know that all the abundant, cheap stuff in the world came into being despite government intervention, taxes, inflation, and borders — not because of them. We know how robust the free market process is and how much better it makes all our lives, despite all attempts to meddle with- and control it.

Praxeology is a remedy for cynics because it can make you appreciate your fellow human beings, and their efforts, more. Many people find the state of the world depressing because they've figured out that governments are generally bad and maybe even that there's something wrong with the money they use. Still, few grasp that the same understanding of how human societies function can make you appreciate productive people more. When you see the whole picture, you begin to appreciate every supermarket cashier, every cleaning lady, and every employee at the car wash more because you understand how they all contribute to the betterment of mankind.

The market produces goods, so ongoing competition establishing who provides the best goods at the lowest prices is a potent motor for progress. The free market and catallactic competition *is* civilization. Everything governments have, they've stolen from productive people. Government produces "bads" instead of goods, so competition for political power has the opposite effect of catallactic competition. In this type of competition, the most unscrupulous win — not those who best adapt to the wants and wishes of their peers.

The study of praxeology offers you insight into human incentives and how they influence what people do. It gives you the tools to understand why listening to what people say is less important than observing what they do. If you want a clearer view of human society and why it is the way it is, you cannot simply look at "evidence." You must understand the ever-changing nature of human wants and wishes and that the only thing we can observe is what actually happened, not what could have been if things were different. The world could have been in a much worse state than it is, but it could also have been in a much better one without government interference making things worse. Understanding human action combined with a basic knowledge of psychology can help you understand the motives of fear-mongers and why they're often successful in promoting their narratives.

Evolutionarily, the human brain developed to pay more attention to news of threats than good news. Taking action when someone yells "Tiger!" benefits your longevity more than when someone yells, "Hey, look at this pretty flower!" The proposed solution to all the threats the alarmists warn us about is always the same — more political control. It doesn't matter whether the perceived threat is terrorists, drugs, weather phenomena, or viruses. For some odd reason, more politics is always the answer. If you've studied human action, you know why. It's all about means and ends. Remember: for the individual actor, the ends always justify the means.

When you see the world more clearly, it becomes easier to separate signal from noise. You can turn your TV off and start contemplating how to acquire more control of your time. You also understand why this is not an egotistical thing to do but rather the best way to improve your situation as well as that of everyone else. You know that freeing up time and accumulating capital are two sides of the same coin. You understand that the division of labor benefits everyone and that focusing on what *you* can do to improve *your* life and the lives of those closest to you is the best way to help the entire planet.

"In the middle of these cogitations, apprehensions, and reflections, it came into my thoughts one day that all this might be a mere chimera of my own."

– Daniel Defoe, *The Life and Adventures of Robinson Crusoe*

17

ARGUMENTATION

CAN science ever derive an ought from an is? It's an age-old question that philosophers have been asking themselves for centuries. The general consensus is "no, it can't," but we can get pretty close using praxeology. Can the proposition "We humans ought not to aggress against one another" hold true scientifically? To answer this question, we must first examine the only non-violent means to arrive at a consensual view of the world, namely argumentation. A conflict arises whenever two people have opposing opinions of who owns what, and the only way to resolve a dispute peacefully is through argumentation. Argumentation is a human action; we can analyze it deductively, like all other human actions. What distinguishes argumentation from other acts is that it is the only non-violent act that can resolve conflicts. Argumentation holds several a-priori truths.

All truth claims are justified and decided upon by argumentation. One cannot dispute this claim since expressing an opposing view would be an attempt to justify one's claim via argumentation. Arguing is purposeful behavior, hence, a human action. In arguing, people use physical means — notably their bodies — to achieve a specific end, an agreement on the *truth value* of a particular proposition. Whether this proposition is objectively true or not is of no matter to the truthfulness of these a-priori statements about argumentation. Even though disagreement drives argumentation, the ultimate goal of the arguing parties is always the same — agreement. Therefore, argumentation is in itself a mutually agreed upon, non-violent interaction between people, aimed at resolving conflict. The validity of the norms of action that make argumentation between two opposing parties possible, in other words, the praxeological presuppositions of argumentation described here, cannot be disputed through argumentation. There are two such presuppositions. In arguing against them, one would again fall into the trap of self-contradiction.

The first praxeological supposition requires that we accept that every one of us owns our bodies. As described earlier, arguing against this is self-contradictory since doing so proves that one is in control of one's body. Some say we have no free will, but this is also a dead end as it would render every deliberate activity useless, including argumentation for or against free will. The second praxeological presupposition of argumentation extends the first — that one owns whatever property one has acquired through acceptable means before the argument begins. As we've learned, a specific relationship between a person and a nature-given object constitutes that person's property. We consider a person the rightful owner of an object when he has interacted with nature to make it or acquired it from someone else through the most common way to acquire property — trade.

Arguing against these presuppositions is as futile as arguing against any other praxeological axiom. In doing so, one demonstrates that one seeks to resolve the issue by arguing in favor of one's position. But suppose one's position suggests that an opponent of the argument is less entitled to the means he is using to argue. In that case, one demonstrates that one does not wish to resolve the conflict by argumentation alone but through some degree of violent means. Not admitting that by arguing, one is verbally battling out the conflict on a leveled playing field would be contrary to the very purpose of argumentation — to resolve the issue peacefully.

Now, can these irrefutable axioms derive an ought from an is? Or at least an *ought not*? In trying to answer this, we have to argue. As shown, one cannot argue against argumentation; consequently, one cannot dispute another person's right to disagree. By arguing, we demonstrate that we believe intellectual argumentation is an appropriate means of resolving conflict. Therefore, we simultaneously display our belief in bodily autonomy and property rights. Holding any other position would be inconsistent and self-contradictory. The praxeological conclusions about argumentation do not prove that one can derive an ought from an is through scientific means. What they *do* prove is that all arguments against self-ownership and absolute property rights are logically inconsistent by definition. Thus, one must subscribe to the idea of property rights to engage in a debate about them.

Because the irrefutable axioms of action and argumentation can be proven true a-priori, all political views that reject absolute individual property rights must be deemed fundamentally false or, at the very least, logically inconsistent. Therefore, there is only one true, logically consistent human right — the right to be left alone. Sadly, we live in a world where these fundamental flaws and inconsistencies prevail — there is no libertarian nation. Moreover, a libertarian nation would be a logical paradox since these principles apply to all human beings, not only those living in a specific geographical area. The ethics of argumentation, however, apply beyond morally consistent libertarian utopias — they are universally applicable to any jurisdiction at any time.

One can not argue against the position that human rights must be universally applicable without contradicting oneself, either. Neither can one deny the validity of argumentation as the only ethical means of arriving at this conclusion without running into contradiction again. Hans-Hermann Hoppe first explained these ethics of argumentation in the 1980s. They constitute one of the most profound yet overlooked scientific and philosophical insights of the last century — that one cannot argue against absolute property rights with intellectual consistency.

Let's illustrate this insight by examining our old friend Robinson Crusoe. Robinson is in possession of his own body. It is impossible to disprove this without contradicting oneself, as one has to argue against any given proposition to prove it untrue. In this case, one would have to, by one's action, show that one was in possession of one's own body to do so, rendering the very act of arguing against the proposition self-contradictory. In short, one has to acknowledge that Robinson has a body to show that he is not in possession of it. Further, it is impossible to say that Robinson is not the rightful owner of his body since doing so would require an equally self-contradictory action. The arguer would thus deny ownership of their own body, rendering the argument invalid for another reason — that the opinion expressed did not belong to the person uttering it.

With bodily possession and ownership resolved, it now follows that Robinson is also the rightful owner of whatever objects he chooses to *appropriate* on the island, simply because no one else is present to claim otherwise. A dispute over ownership can only arise when two or more people are present. Enter Friday. As Friday arrives on the island, he can now claim that an object that Robinson possesses rightfully belongs to him instead. The only peaceful means Friday has to get Robinson to give him said object is to argue that it belongs to him. To deny this would, once again, be an act of self-contradiction. Therefore, original appropriation as the correct means of figuring out ownership rights is irrefutable. Similarly, it is equally indisputable that Friday would be the object's rightful owner had he voluntarily exchanged it with Robinson for some other good or favor.

To elaborate further, imagine that Friday one day forcefully enslaves Robinson. Even in this situation, argumentation is perfectly possible. An argument about something arbitrary, like the amount of fish remaining in the pond on a particular day, could be carried out, leading to an agreement between Friday and Robinson. But any argument about the morality of one person treating the other as his property would inevitably lead to contradiction unless it leads to the immediate emancipation of the enslaved individual. Today, we can trace almost all property ownership back to voluntary as well as involuntary exchanges throughout human history. It is virtually impossible to say that any particular object rightfully belongs to a specific person because to do that, one would have to investigate the actual ownership of all the factors of production that played a role in its creation since the beginning of civilization. Because this is practically impossible, we focus on future conduct and who owns what in the present.

The only way to peacefully establish who is the legitimate owner of a particular object in the present is to argue about it. In light of this fact, we can conclude that a politician can debate the validity of a tax, but as long as the taxed live under threats of punishment if they refuse to pay their taxes, all pro-taxation arguments are invalid. Probably so. If the taxman and his victim cannot resolve their dispute by agreeing with one another, they are no longer equals but in a master-slave relationship. And if the relationship devolves into slave and master, any argument between them is not an actual argument but a mockery on behalf of the enslaver.

Your government is mocking you whenever it says it has given you a "right" to do something. The only thing it can "give" you is temporary permission to do something. All a government can do is take things away from you. As long as some entity "governs" you without your consent, you're a slave. You're only free to do one thing — obey. Anyone claiming anything else is misguided, confused, brainwashed, or outright evil and mocking you. All arguments against these irrefutable truths are self-contradictory and, ultimately, invalid.

"Upon the whole, here was an undoubted testimony that there was scarce any condition in the world so miserable but there was something negative or something positive to be thankful for in it."

– Daniel Defoe, *The Life and Adventures of Robinson Crusoe*

18

CONCLUSION

HUMAN ACTION is purposeful behavior, and praxeology is the study of human action. It can give you insights into how practically everything in human society works and point out the limits of what we can and cannot know about ourselves and our interactions. The conclusions drawn from praxeology may paint a bleak picture of the present state of human affairs, but accepting reality is always a necessary precursor to knowledge. Moreover, while praxeology can expose the true nature of governments, it also explains how much of a force for good the free market process truly is. Praxeology illuminates how humans cooperating voluntarily for selfish reasons ultimately brings prosperity and abundance to all. It can kindle hope in the hearts of cynics, revitalizing their appreciation for other people.

Every supermarket clerk, every car mechanic, every cleaning lady, and even every YouTuber plays their part in the market process. Even public sector employees play a role in the market. We all act as producers, consumers, capitalists, and entrepreneurs at different stages of our lives, regardless of whether money is involved or not. We all act with intent. We all speculate because the future is never certain. We have no choice but to try to improve our lives out of our own free will. Acting on purpose is what being human is. So mind your own business, don't steal, and start doing something. We'll all be better off if you do.

This is the way.

Further Reading

Human Action by Ludwig Von Mises

The Ethics of Liberty by Murray N. Rothbard

Anatomy of the State by Murray N. Rothbard

A Theory of Capitalism and Socialism by Hans-Hermann Hoppe

Economic Science and the Austrian Method by Hans-Hermann Hoppe

The Sovereign Individual by William Rees-Mogg & James Dale Davidson

The Austrian School for Investors by Rahim Taghizadegan & Ronald Stoferle

The Emperor's New Clothes by Hans Christian Andersen

1984 by George Orwell

Animal Farm by George Orwell

Brave New World by Aldous Huxley

Atlas Shrugged by Ayn Rand

The Life and Adventures of Robinson Crusoe by Daniel Defoe

The White Pill by Michael Malice

Index

A
A-posteriori, 1, 2, 48, 73, 74
A-priori, 1, 2, 12, 13, 25, 44, 48, 74, 90, 100, 113, 115
Age of Enlightenment, 73
Altruism, 24, 54, 59
Asterix and Obelix, 30
Austrian Method, 44, 121

B
Balance sheet, 38
Biological competition, 51, 53, 56

C
Cantillon effect, 109
Capital, 24, 27, 29, 45–47, 53, 54, 59–63, 66–68, 81, 88–90, 93–95, 99, 100, 102, 103, 108, 110
Capital accumulation, 27, 29, 65–69, 75, 88, 89, 99
Capital goods, 25, 27, 29, 39, 43, 46, 60–62, 65–67, 71, 75, 89, 93–95, 100–102
Capitalism, 40, 43, 47, 55, 63, 66, 95, 121
Catallactic, 45, 51, 53, 56, 60, 65, 69, 72, 90, 94, 109, 110
Catallactic competition, 51
Catallactics, 43, 51
Citizen Kane, 40
Civilization, 4, 29–31, 37, 48, 63, 73, 99, 109, 116
CPI, 81

D
Delayed gratification, 22, 28, 100
Democracy, 47
Disutility of labor, 22
Divisibility, 35–37
Division of labor, 30–32, 35, 37, 53, 54, 72, 110
Double coincidence of wants, 35, 37

E
Economic calculation, 37–40, 43, 47, 48, 54, 72, 79, 82, 108
Empirical, 1, 2, 17, 25, 39, 44, 48, 69, 73, 74, 85, 90
Entrepreneurship, 39, 46, 47, 59–63, 65–67, 71–73, 79, 93–95, 100–102, 119

F
Factors of production, 17, 18, 27, 72, 73, 94, 96, 100, 116
Felt uneasiness, 4, 9, 15, 49, 59
Fiat currency, 41, 82, 83, 108
First principle, 2, 4, 48
Free market, 10, 24, 32, 43, 45, 47, 48, 51–53, 55, 60, 61, 63, 65, 67, 68, 71, 74–76, 79, 82, 83, 99, 103, 107, 109, 119
Friday, 30–32, 36, 38, 47, 54, 62, 116

G
Government produced "bads", 110

H

Hans-Hermann Hoppe, 115, 121
Horizontal widening, 101
Human action, 1–4, 9, 11, 12, 17, 25, 29,
    43, 45, 48, 53, 55, 59, 60, 71,
    73, 74, 86, 88, 90, 110, 113, 119

I

Inflation, 37, 67, 81–83, 103, 107–109
Interest, 76, 94–96, 99–101, 103, 107, 108
Intrinsic value, 43

J

James Bond, 65

K

Keynesianism, 108

L

Labor, 17, 20–25, 27, 30–32, 35, 37, 39, 53,
    54, 66, 67, 72, 85, 86, 89,
    93–95, 99, 102
Lamborghini, 40
Law of Returns, 18
Leisure, 21–23, 25, 41, 46, 80, 86
Ludwig von Mises, 2, 73

M

Malinvestment, 38
Marginal utility, 15, 16, 22, 24, 79, 80, 89
Market intervention, 45, 67, 69, 76, 102
Medium of exchange, 35, 36, 46, 72, 79,
    82, 83
Monetary good, 36, 82, 83, 87
Money, 4, 9, 25, 35–41, 43–46, 48, 51, 60,
    62, 66–68, 72, 75, 76, 78–83,
    86–88, 92–96, 100–104,
    107–109, 119
Money Regression Theorem, 82
Monopoly, 61, 75, 76, 88

N

Nature-given means, 27

O

Opportunity cost, 39, 85, 95

P

Prices, 13, 17, 37–41, 46, 47, 51, 60, 61,
    66–68, 71–73, 75, 76, 79–82,
    90, 94–96, 100–104, 108, 109
Profit, 39–41, 44, 46, 59–63, 66, 71–73, 75,
    79, 90, 94, 100, 102
Propaganda, 25, 55, 74

Q

Quantitative easing, 108

R

Renewable energy, 69
Ricardian Law of Association, 31, 54
Richard M. Nixon, 107
Robinson Crusoe, xii, 1, 8, 10, 14–16,
    18–20, 25–32, 34, 36, 38, 42,
    44, 47, 50, 52, 54, 58, 62, 64,
    67, 70, 78, 80, 84, 88, 89, 92,
    98, 100–102, 106, 112, 115,
    116, 118, 121

S

Saleability, 25, 36, 37, 79
Saving, 4, 27, 29, 35, 36, 46, 47, 65, 68, 69,
    78, 87, 94, 99–102
Self-ownership, 115
Social science, 1, 2, 53
Structure of Production, 27

T

Taxes, 25, 48, 52, 67, 69, 83, 87, 90, 108,
    109, 117
The Beatles, 40
The Broken Window Fallacy, 45
The duration of serviceability, 86
The market, 30, 32, 36, 43, 47, 51–54, 60,
    65, 66, 68, 71, 75, 93, 95, 96,
    100, 101, 103, 107, 108, 119
The period of production, 85
Time preference, 28, 54, 80, 87–90,
    93–95, 99, 100, 102, 103, 107
Truth value, 113

V

Vertical deepening, 101
Voting, 47